TRANSACTIO
BURGON SOCIETY

Volume 23   2023

Published October 2024

1   Officers
2   Events
3   Fellows and Members

9   A Tribute to Nicholas Groves
13   Editor's Note
131   Authors
133   Shop

Primary Source: Philip Goff
15   The Development of the Burgon Society Hoods

Bruce Christianson, Philip Goff, and Nicholas Groves
23   Capuciis Furruratis cum Serico Duplicatis: Furred Hoods with Silk Linings from the Late Nineteenth Century

Andrew Plant
39   Designing in Circles, Conversing in Triangles, Dressing in Squares: Evolving the Academic Dress of the University of Sussex, 1958–1963

Edward Teather
75   The History of Undergraduate Academical Dress in Britain's Modern Universities since 1880, with a Discussion of its Recent and Current Use

Samuel Teague
94   The Contemporary Usage of Academic Hoods in Oxford Collegiate Choirs

Peter A. Thompson
110   An Odd Habit: A Study of the Use of the Academic Hood in the Portraits of the Archbishops of Armagh

TRANSACTIONS OF THE BURGON SOCIETY

Volume 23 (for 2023)
Published October 2024
newprairiepress.org/burgonsociety

Published by The Burgon Society
© 2024 The Contributors
burgon.org.uk

ISBN 978-1-8380679-7-7
Printed in England

The Burgon Society

Officers

(as at 1 August 2024)

President

Professor Graham Zellick, CBE, KC, MA, PhD (Cantab), Hon LLD (Birmingham & American International University), LHD (New York), DLit (QMUL), AcSS, Hon FRAM, Hon FSALS, FBS

Executive Committee (Trustees)

Chairman Andrew Hogg, MA (Dublin), MSc (Toronto), PhD (Aberdeen), CGeol, FGS, FBS

Secretary Alice Hynes, BA (Exeter), MA (London), FCIS, MAPM, MInstLM, FAUA, FRSA, FBS

Treasurer Terry Barcock, BSc (Bradford), MBA (Open), FFSC, FRSA, FBS

Ordinary Members

Jonathan C. Cooper, BSc (St Andrews), PhD (Central Lancs), FRGS, FBS *(Dean of Studies)*

The Reverend Philip F. M. Goff, BD (London), AKC, FSA, FBS *(Convenor, Research Advisory Group)*

Valentina S. Grub, BA (Wellesley College), MLitt, PhD (St Andrews), FBS *(Editor, Burgon Notes)*

Nicola Hardy, MA (Cantab), FBS

John C. Horton, BSc (Manchester), PhD (Cantab), MInstP, FBS *(Marshal)*

Nicholas Jackson, BA (York), MSc, PhD (Warwick), FBS

Andrew Plant, BA (Leeds), PhD (Birmingham), FBS *(Webmaster)*

Chris Williams, MA (Cantab), MA (Colchester Inst.), FBS *(Curator)*

Professor Stephen L. Wolgast, BA (Kansas State), MS (Columbia), FBS *(Publications Officer and Editor of Transactions)*

Burgon Society Events in 2023

4 March **Virtual speaker event**
Online via Zoom

Peter Campbell — *Distinctive or Derivative: The Development of Doctoral Dress in Australia*

22 April **Spring Conference and AGM**
Deloitte LLP, London, EC4A 3TR

Programme included the AGM and the following talks:

Bruce Christianson *The Original PhD Robes at the University of London (And What Happened Next)*

Neil Dickson *Interlude: An Oxford DPhil Convocation Habit*

Andrew Hogg *The Swedish Convention for Academic Ceremonies Visit to Trinity College Dublin, 21 March 2023*

John Horton *Robing Rooms, Maces, Gowns and Bureaucracy … 20 Years in the Life of a Nottingham University Marshal*

Mike Ratcliffe *A Quickening in the Pace of Change in UK University Graduation Ceremonies in the Last 5 Years*

Samuel Teague *Contemporary Usage of Academic Hoods in Oxford Collegiate Choirs*

4 June **Virtual speaker event**
Online via Zoom

Jonas Kågström *A Lutheran Peacock: The Development of Swedish Academic Dress*

12 August **Garden Party**
Octagon Unitarian Chapel & Martineau Hall, 21a Colegate, Norwich NR3 1BN

3 September **Virtual speakers' event**
Online via Zoom

Two presentations on Ghanaian academic dress in association with the University of Education, Winneba, Ghana:

Peggy Simpson *Investigation into the Design History of Academic Gowns of Selected Technical Universities in Ghana*

Osuanyi Quaicoo Essel *Academic Gown Designs in Ghana: An Aesthetic Discourse of Patrick Osei-Poku's Decolonial Efforts*

8 October	**Congregation** University of Chester
	Admission to the Fellowship of the Burgon Society
	Michael Bunton (by submission — Decently and in Order: The Warham Guild Hood)
	Anthony Johnson (by submission — John Rous: Don, Divine or Dandy? Determining Academic Dress as Distinct from the Clerical — and the Civil from Both — in 15th-Century England, with Particular Reference to the University of Oxford)
	Andrew Plant (by submission — Designing in Circles, Conversing in Triangles, Dressing in Squares: Tracing the Evolution of the Academical Dress of the University of Sussex 1958–1966)
	Liran Renert (by submission — Coats of Many Colours: A Brief Review of Academic Dress in Israel)
	Samuel Teague (by submission — The Contemporary Usage of Academic Hoods in Oxford Collegiate Choirs)
	Programme included the following
	The Revd Philip Goff *A Tribute to Dr Nicholas Groves, FBS, FRHistS*
	Debbie Newns, University of Chester *Chester Academic Dress and Ceremonial*
	Ian Sudlow-McKay, Napier Univ *Chester Dress: A View from On-stage and Off*
	Nicola Hardy, University of Cambridge *Cambridge Ceremonial Tales*
	Charles Tsua *Gimp, Lace & Braid: New Developments and Discoveries*
15 December	**Virtual speaker event** Online via Zoom
	Nicholas Rowe *The Doctoral Sword of Finland: Tracing an Academy's Right to Bear Arms*

Fellows and Members
(as at 1 August 2024)

Fellows
Indicates fellow-elect
+Indicates a Fellow without voting rights

Mr Robert Armagost +

Professor Sir John Baker +
Dr Richard Baker
Mr David J. P. Baldwin
Mr Terry Barcock*
Dr Andrew-John Bethke +
Sqn Ldr Alan Birt +
Mr Christopher Bottley
Dr David T. Boven
Mr Michael Brewer +
Dr Giles Brightwell
Mr Ronald Brookes +
Dr Michael Bunton

Mr Stephen Callander +
Mr Arthur B. Casey
The Rt Revd and Rt Hon.
    Lord Chartres +
Professor Peter Chiu +
Professor Bruce Christianson
Mr Peter W. Clarke
Dr Jonathan C. Cooper
The Revd Dr Noel S. B. Cox
Dr Paul Robert Coxon
The Revd Kenneth Ian Crawford

The Revd Dr Graham Deans
Dr Neil Kay Dickson
Mrs Kathryn Douglas +
Dr Donald L. Drakeman
The Revd Matthew Duckett +
Mr Peter Durant

The Revd Edmund J. Eggleston
Dr Michael W. Everett

Mr Paul Fielder
Mr Colin A. M. Fleming
Ms Kerstin Fröberg

Professor William Thomas Gibson

Dr Nicholas Gledhill
The Revd Philip Goff
Mr Thomas Anthony Goodman +
Professor John N. Grant
Dr Valentina S. Grub

Professor Martin Hardcastle
The Revd Dr John James Harding
Mrs Nicola Hardy
The Revd Seamus Addison Hargrave
Dr Thorsten Hauler +
Mr Paul Anthony Hayward
Dr Nicholas Gray Heavens
Lieutenant Nicholas A. Hoffmann +
Dr Andrew J. C. Hogg
Dr John Charles Horton
Miss Alice Ruth Hynes

Dr Nicholas James Jackson
The Revd Canon Dr Stephen James
Mr Anthony Johnson
Mr Ian A. Johnson

Dr Michael Kearsley +
The Revd Father Oliver James Keenan
Dr Alex Kerr
The Rt Revd Graeme Knowles
Mr Charles Ka Shing Ko +
The Very Revd Harry E. Krauss

Mr Martin Lewis
The Revd Jack Lindsay
Mr Philip Lowe
Dr John Lundy +

Professor Yves Mausen
The Revd Douglas MacMillan*
Mr Timothy Nicholas Milner
Dr Simon James Morris

Mr Brian Morley Newman
Professor Leonard E. Newton

Dr Andrew James Peter North
Dr Susan North

Mr David Parker
Mr Scott Pilkington
Dr Steven E. Plank
Dr Andrew M. Plant
Dr Michael Powell

Mr David Christopher Quy

Dr Byron W. Rangiwai +
Mr Liran Renert
Professor Aileen Ribeiro +
Mr Edward Ripley
Dr Leslie M. M. Robarts
Dr Alan J. Ross +
Dr Nicholas Rowe

Dr Matthew Cheung Salisbury +
Miss Elizabeth Scott
Mr Nick Shipp +
Professor Klaus Solberg Søilen +
Professor Kenneth L. Suit, Jr

Mr Samuel G. Teague
Mr Jason T. Testar +
The Venerable Dr Peter Thompson*
Dr James P. S. Thomson
Mr Charles Rupert Tsua

Mr Philip Edward Waters
Dr Sandra Wearden
Mr Chris Williams
Professor Stephen L. Wolgast

Mr Alexander K. Yen

Professor Graham J. Zellick

Deceased Fellows
Dr John Birch, *died 2012*
The Revd Dr John Lester Brennan, *died 2023*
Mr Leonard Brown, *died 2007*
Mr Clifford Dunkley, *died 2019*
Dr Nicholas Groves, *died 2023*
Dr Francis Jackson, *died 2022*
Dr John Lancaster, *died 2023*
Professor Bruno Neveu, *died 2004*
Mr Mitchell Anderson Nicholls, *died 2023*
The Revd Dr Steven A. Peay, *died 2020*
Dr Robin Rees, *died 2021*
Dr George Wenham Shaw, *died 2006*
Dr Mary Shaw, *died 2022*
The Revd Canon Ambrose Southward, *died 2019*
Mr John Venables, *died 2021*

Members
Mr Emmanuel (Abiodun) Adekoya
Dr Christopher Ahlstrom
Dr Malcolm Aickin
Dr Christian Anderson
Mr James Douglas Anderson
Mr David Annabale
Amb. Andrzej Antoszkiewicz
Mr Nicholas Arnold

Jayne Ball Designs
Mr Paul Barber

The Very Revd Tim Barker
Dr John J. Barnes
The Revd Dr Anthony M. Barratt
Mr David C. M. Barton
Professor Gary Francis Baxter
Mr John Bishop
Mr John Blake
The Revd Dr Andrew Blume
The Revd Dr Christian D. Boyd
Mr Thomas W. Brian

The Very Revd Dr Godfrey Brown
Mr Graeme Bruce
Mr Ian James Burton

Mr Neil Kay Cameron
Mr Alexander Campbell
Mr Jimmy Campbell
Dr Peter Campbell
Mrs Morwenna Campbell-Smith
Mr Leslie Carrick-Smith
Churchill Gowns
Mr Peter Mark Close
The Revd Jonathan Collis
Mr William Collison
Mr Jeremy Colman
Mr William G. Condé
Mr Martin Cooke
Mr Craig Copley-Brown
The Revd Ivor Cornish
Mrs Janette Corporal
Cosprop Ltd
Mr Shane Creppel
Mr Michael Crouch
The Revd Dr James Curry

Canon Adrian Daffern
Mr John Dalton
Professor James H. Davenport
Mr Andrew Mark Davidson
Dr Josu de la Fuente
Dr Sebastian De Line
Mr Antti de Ruano
Mr Simon James Deitlmeier
Dr Paul Devlin
The Revd Canon Dr Michael Diamond
Mr Andrew Jan Dobrzanski
Mr Thomas Dobson
Mr William Done
The Revd Andrew Peter Doohan
Mr James Anthony Drabble
Dr Michael A. K. Duggan
Dr Jason Dunn
Mr Geoffrey Dye

Mr Matthew James Edwards
Ede & Ravenscroft Ltd
Dr Paul Ellison
The Revd Dr David Roderick Evans
The Revd Dr Keith James Eyeons

Mr Benjamin Francis Falcon
Mr James George Fearon

Dr Leslie Fife
Mr Alexander Fitch-Holland
Professor Anthony William Fox
Mr David Salsbery Fry
Dr Heinz Fuchs

Dr Stephen Gallagher
Mr Thomas M. Garrett
Mr Edmund Hugh Gazeley
Dr Markus Gehring
Mr Roberto Gherseni
Mr Cameron Giles
Dr Peter John Gorton
Gowning Street Pty Ltd
Cdr Peter Gracey
Graduate Gowning Company
Graduation Attire
Mr Elijah Z. Granet
Mr Hayden Gray
Dr Walter G. Green
The Revd Canon Mark N. Gretason
Mr Leslie Grout

Mr Christopher J. Ha
Mr Morgan Hale
Mr Timothy James Benedict Hallett
Dr Patrick Hampshire
Mr Patrick Martin Harrigan
Civis Taneli Heinänen
The Revd Gregory Henderson
Mr John Hill
Mr Samuel Hill
Mr Peter Edward Holden
Mr Jamie Holland
Mr Ian Martin Howard
Mr Jake Humbles
Mr Garry Paul Humphreys
Mr Paul Stephen Hunt
Mr Paul Hutchings

His Excellency Julius Jackson
Dr Colin Graeme Johnson
The Revd Anthony J. L. Jones, *died 2023*
Mr Harley Jones
Professor Jonathan Jones
Dr Mark Alexander Goddard Jones

Dr Jonas Kågström
Professor Stephen F. Keevil
The Revd B. David Kennedy
Dr Lloyd James Peter Kilford
The Revd George Kilpatrick

Mr Thomas Francis King
Dr Caroline Knight
Dr Francis Knights
His Honour Judge Graham Roy Knowles
Mr Michael Kolcun II
Dr Nikolas Krawchenko
Mr Fabian Krougman

Dr Philip John Lankester
The Revd Dr William Roy Large
Mr Martin Lawrence
The Revd Father Edward Lewis
Mr Kenson Li
The Rt Hon The Lord Lingfield
Professor Benedikt Loewe
Mr James Lyons

Marston Robing Ltd
Mr Jack Mason
The Revd James Mather
Canon Brian McKay
Mr Andrew McKeown
Mr Callum McLeod
Ms Liz McMahan
Professor Thomas McSweeney
Mr Dennis Shane Miller
The Revd Christopher James Mogridge
Mr Rhys James David Mott
Mr Roger Moult
The Revd Graeme Watson McKinnon
    Muckart
Dr Keith Munday

Mr Nathaniel Nagar
Mr Behroz Sasan Nanevasadeh
The Revd Robin Nash
Mr Gareth Neame
Dr Roderick Forsyth Neilson
Mr H. G. Gordon Nevill ++
The Revd Dr Peter Newing
Dr Stuart Newton
Dr Andrew Nicoll
Mr Jeremy Nigel Fortescue Norman
William Northam & Co. Ltd
Dr Richard Num

Mr Mark Ockenden
Dr Gustavo Adolfo Ornelas-Almaraz

Cdr Thomas Packer

————————————

++ *Indicates an Honorary Member*

M. Perkins & Son Ltd
Mr Benjamin Francis Phillips
Mr Mervyn Howard Pilley
Mr Shawn Pinette
Dr Andrew Pink
Mr Adam Prieur
The Revd Anthony F. Pybus

Mr Mike Ratcliffe
Ms Mary Rauchfuss
The Revd Anthony Reader-Moore
Dr Richard Philip Reece
Mr Steven Rhodes
Mr Robin Richardson
Dr Jakob K. Rinderknecht
Dr Sarah Elin Roberts
Mr Alan S. Robertson
Robes of Distinction
Mr MSTR Rogers
Mr Timothy Charles Roll-Pickering

The Revd Professor Charles Shaw
The Revd Norman William Shaw
Shepherd & Woodward Group
Dr Giles Shilson
Mr Kyle Siwek
Dr Harry Spillane
Mr Kevin William Stone
Mr Ian Stuart Henry Sudlow-McKay
Dr Martin Sunnqvist
Mr Jacob Switzer

The Very Revd Michael E. Tavinor
Mr Stewart Lee Thompson
Mr Benjamin Francis Titmus
Mr Julian A. Torres-H-Bonilla
Mr Brian Turvey

The University of Chester

Mr Richard Maria van der Beek

Dr Geoffrey D. Wandesforde-Smith
The Revd Dr Robin Ward
The Revd David Warner
The Revd Dr Derek Herbert Webster ++
Dr Michael Wells
The Hon. Richard Whitaker
Mr Ivo Wiesendanger
Ass.Jur. Sandro Wiggerich
Mr Anthony George Willenbruch
Dr Huw Williams
Dr Jon Williams

The Revd Canon Dr Paul Rhys Williams
Dr Robert B. Williams
Professor Michael Willis
Dr Patrick Wills
Dr Jamie Wilmore
J. Wippell & Co. Ltd, *closed 2023*
Professor Marcin Wiszowaty
Mr Isaac Wong
Dr David Andrew Woolf
Mr Peter Worby
Dr Charles Wynne-Jones

The Revd Ian Ira Yemm

Transactions of the Burgon Society, 23 (2023), pages 9–11

A Tribute to Nicholas Groves

By Philip Goff

It is almost impossible to imagine the academic dress world without Nick Groves, such was his contribution to it from high up in his Norfolk tower, that was certainly not ivory! And that contribution was so immense that he will live on forever, linked with Shaw, the brilliant Groves Classification Scheme, and the founding of this Society, in which he played a major part, as its first Dean, and as a Council member until 2011.

In the mid-1960s, aged fourteen, I already knew of all the robemakers in the British Isles, and was in regular correspondence with most of them. Then, and later in the decade, on visits to the academic tailors based in London and Cambridge, the name, Nicholas Groves, was mentioned regularly, and I was intrigued that there should be anyone else in the known universe with a similar interest; and it was not long before we made contact.

So it was that an acquaintanceship, then friendship, was born, that has spanned more than half a century. In the early 1970s, as part of my training for ordination, I spent a blissful year in Norwich, living, for part of the time, in the Cathedral Close. Thus, it was impossible not to know one of its most devoted sons, and we found that we had many mutual friends.

Of course, in those days we wrote letters and reserved telephone calls for urgent matters, but during my time as Academic Consultant at Ede & Ravenscroft, from 1996, Nick and I began to meet more frequently, and the burgeoning internet, and use of email, had become established, changing forever the way people communicate. For work, and for interest, I had begun to make regular searches for anything connected to academic dress. This was an easy task since the pages numbered in the low hundreds. As I wrote this, a quick check revealed some 530,000,000 of them.

On discovering Br Michael Powell's lone SETI-like message, on his newly formed Yahoo academic dress eGroup, in 1999, and with great excitement, the very first thing I did, after responding to Michael, was to tell Nick Groves. From that time onwards, and as others joined us, we were in frequent contact: sharing knowledge; sparking ideas; hatching plans; moaning about the fading quality of the robes of yesteryear; complaining about the liberties taken by robemakers and sharing information on publications and textiles as well as news of new, obscure or defunct hoods.

From the outset of those contacts and meetings it was clear that Nick was hugely talented. Widely read, erudite, scholarly, articulate, opinionated, unusual, amusing, a little old-worldly, perhaps, he was a one-off and, in more than one sense of the word, nonconformist. He was a gifted musician, antiquarian, historian, teacher, linguist and, perhaps, even theologian.

Fr Goff delivered this tribute at the 2023 Congregation at the University of Chester in October.

As an alumnus of London, Wales, York and East Anglia universities, he might equally have pursued a successful career teaching history, or music, or English, or the Welsh language or theology (I suspect this list is not exhaustive), but although he was a teacher for a while, and a lecturer, subsequently, he never really fitted into a mould, but was a genuine free thinker.

In another person this combination of academic gifts might have led to a certain dryness and introspection but, coupled with Nick's personality, it led to a rich and generous outpouring of knowledge and wisdom, readily shared with his huge circle of colleagues, friends, devotees, disciples and the upcoming generation of academic dress enthusiasts. He wore his learning lightly, however, and his humour and outrageiosity (if there is such a word) threatened to break out at any moment. He was the David Starkey of academic dress, at once erudite and naughty: a mixture of solid learning and high campery.

Words fascinated him and his vocabulary was rich and wide. 'Nugatory' was one of his favourites, along with 'recondite' and he had some unusual turns of phrase which were his hallmark. 'Hello Nick', I would say on the phone, 'I did a new design for Ede's last week.' 'Did you though?' he would reply. He was a true one-off.

Underneath his learning and solid research, into the subject we all love, was his enjoyment of it all and a huge sense of fun. I cannot emphasise enough, to the present day custodians of our Society, how important a driver this having fun was for us all, and how we founders wished this to continue. Indeed, the agreement given by colleagues, in our pre-Burgon academic dress group, to my desire to see our hobby grounded in a formal society, was only finally given on the condition that we continued to have fun and not become another dreary organisation, hidebound by management speak and corporate nonsense. In this Nick was an enormous support and he understood completely the need to balance scholarship with enjoyment.

With regard to academic dress, Nick had an encyclopaedic knowledge of virtually every scheme in existence in the UK and far beyond. His workbooks illustrating the academic hoods of various universities, hand-coloured and presenting them all together on a page, were wonderful to see and conceived long before robemakers picked up the idea, using sophisticated software. Fortunately, they are now available to us and to posterity in our splendid archive. Moreover, his invention of the Groves Classification of Academic Dress is brilliant in its conception and simplicity and has allowed aficionados, robemakers and students of the subject to communicate more easily.

Enthusiastic and supportive, from the very beginning, of the idea of forming a society for the enjoyment, promotion and formal study of academic dress, he also gave it the name 'Burgon' and when the inevitable fellowship hood was adopted, out of a large list of contenders, he found a brilliant way of connecting the colours to the life of the eponymous Dean.

Nick served as the first Dean of Studies of the Burgon Society and did the spadework for its constitution, largely drawing on that of the Royal Historical Society, of which he was also a fellow.

Publications followed, which are important contributions and will become even more important as the years go by: music colleges, theological colleges, Shaw, *Transactions*, and all the while working and researching for his doctorate on Norwich churches, at Lampeter, University of Wales, for which he was offered the choice of the faculties of Arts or Theology and chose Theology because he liked the red shot blue silk and already had the MA with the blue shot green.

There was so much more to come and his death is a huge loss.

Interestingly, for one so fascinated by university costume, Nick had no time for dressing up (except it be in a gown and hood). He refused to own a suit and, like Dr Franklyn, as Nick tells us in his recent book on the irascible physician, wouldn't attend functions at which very formal dress was required. He also wasn't pompous about academic dress and refused to condemn some of the rather spurious societies which sprang up, each of them with their garish gowns and hoods. Indeed, he designed costumes for many of them, and some he had created himself, such as his Norwich University, through which he awarded degrees to several of his friends. I like to think that Burgon reined him in a little and gave that brilliant mind a forum in which to focus his talents.

His flat in Norwich was a sort of cross between the London Library and a robe-maker's stockroom, surrounded as he was with books, and boxes and boxes of hoods, bought, borrowed, given, some he had made himself and some from his own designs.

Visits to him in Norwich were always full of laughter, such as that made by Bruce Christianson, Paul Coxon and me, last November. The visits were a sort of liturgy and followed a form, as first we sat in a pub putting the world to rights. Then the walk through Town, via the Cathedral, to sticky buns and tea at his place, with the inevitable hood fondling, all along commenting on what had once been where and what was being built. He was a natural guide and what he didn't know about Norwich was not worth knowing.

His health deteriorated rapidly in early 2023: his back began to play up and some of his emails began to be rather vague. Eventually, it dawned that something was up. Not hearing from him for a couple of weeks, I mailed him in early June. His reply was prescient: 'the back's a bit better thanks, but I feel terminally fatigued.' None of us foresaw quite what was happening, and the end was swift.

We have much to think about as a Society by way of preserving his work and honouring his memory, but for now, farewell Nick, thank you for all the scholarship and laughter. God bless you and thank you.

Editor's Note

Rules endure only as long as they are followed. Even when they are written down and codified, they lose their effectiveness when we ignore them. In these pages you will read of dress, academic and otherwise, that changed despite the rules in the University of Sussex, in Oxford's collegiate choirs, and in the portraits of the archbishops of Armagh.

Another change to academic dress happened in the US. The Academic Costume Code, the successor to the 1895 Intercollegiate Code that governed American academic dress, is no more.

I was surprised this summer when, after seeing a social media post that made me want to review the American rules, I searched for them on the site of their sponsor I found this message: 'The American Council on Education no longer hosts information about academic regalia and ceremonies, as current policies vary.'[1]

What happened? A phone call in July to the Council's director of public affairs, Audrey Hamilton, yielded some details. The Council decided to end its connection with cap and gown around 2022, she said, because the person on the Council's staff who had fielded questions had retired, leaving no one qualified to answer incoming queries.

Changes beyond the Council's roster contributed to the decision. Hamilton pointed out that colleges and universities had been doing what they wanted with academic dress. With less attention to the Code, its importance dwindled.

Whether its demise should be mourned or celebrated is another question, and the reality that its passing went unnoticed for two years by so many of us tells the real story. Universities and society have changed immeasurably since the first Code identified the eight fields of education. One set of rules for 4,000 universities just didn't work.

Allowing each college to select its own scheme of academic dress in the twenty-first century reflects the way Americans dress today, with the emphasis on individuality rather than membership in a group. As early as 1967, the Council's costume committee noted that 'it is impossible (and probably undesirable) to lay down enforceable rules', and over the years departures grew.[2] Most bachelors' gowns, for example, lost their pointed sleeves many years ago. When it comes to trim colour, virtually no university or robemaker could agree whether the hood's should reflect the name of the degree (Arts, for example) or the field of study (such as Music)—Kenneth Suit Jr.'s work in *Transactions* Volumes 15, 18 and 21 notwithstanding.

To Americans who actually paid attention to the Code, variations like these could be maddening. To those who worried that the Code risked making fossils of academic dress, its end is a relief.[3]

When its wearers change academic dress, it remains a living thing, growing and evolving to meet changing needs.   —*Stephen Wolgast*

---

1   American Council on Education, 'Academic Regalia and Ceremonies,' at <www.acenet.edu/Programs-Services/Pages/Regalia-Redirect.aspx> [retrieved 25 August 2024].

2   Memo, 'Regulations affecting academic costume,' from the Commission on Academic Affairs, ACE, to 'Member institutions,' 9 November 1967, Columbia University in the City of New York, University Archives. See also David T. Boven, 'American Universities' Departure from the Academic Costume Code', *TBS*, 9 (2009), pp. 156–74.

3   See Nicholas Groves and Bruce Christianson, 'Wearing Mummy's Clothes: An Introduction to Academical Archaeology', *TBS*, 4 (2004), pp. 42–43.

Transactions of the Burgon Society, 23 (2023), pages 15–22

The Development of the Burgon Society Hoods

The [s2] was straightforward, but the [f7] had a more dramatic inception, *Philip Goff writes*

It is unsurprising that a society set up for the study and enjoyment of academic dress would devote some time to discussion of costumes for its members. The truth is, however, that there was much else to do in the early years of the Society, and creating something that would be taken seriously, at least in the world of costume and dress studies, was uppermost in the minds of the founders. Of course, we had no shortage of ideas and plenty of experience, elsewhere, of dry-as-dust committees and proce-

___

Primary Source
Wherein a Fellow's expertise and the outside world meet

___

dures that we had no wish to replicate. In fact, the early Burgon meetings were full of fun and laughter and when we did get round to discussing costume, as might be expected, there was an abundance of proposals.

A supplement to the twentieth-anniversary volume of *Transactions* records the advent of the Society's official and academic costume along with a record of how the Society was formed in 2000.[1] The specification for the Burgon Society Fellows' hood was agreed at a Council meeting in January 2001.

The FBS Congregation hood

Made in a generously cut Burgon [s2] shape,[2] the Fellows' Congregation hood has a shell of black corded silk or artificial silk. Its pink lining fabric is known, in the robe-making business, as judges' ruby and is a shot silk which has a crimson weft woven on an ivory white warp.[3] The silk takes its name from the sleeve linings of the robes of the Bailiff of Guernsey, as can be seen in the portrait of Sir Peter Stafford Carey, Kt. (1803–86) (Fig. 1), and in the photo of HM King Charles with the current Bailiff (Fig. 2). The silk is also seen on the facings on the cuffs of the robes worn by the jurats, or judges of that island.[4]

As an admirer of this particular silk for many years, I wanted to preserve its use and was able to incorporate it into the new University of London specialist doctors' robes designed for Ede & Ravenscroft Ltd, in 1997 (Fig. 3).

The ruby shot silk was woven by Stephen Walters & Sons Ltd, of Sudbury, a company, founded in 1720, that grew out of the exodus of the Spitalfields silk weavers, who settled on the Essex/Suffolk borders in the mid-nineteenth century. Over many years

---

1 Philip Goff, *Hoods by the Armful* (London: Burgon Society, 2021).
2 There was never any doubt as to which shape would be used!
3 The warp colour is described in the trade as 'natural'.
4 After 1635 High Court Judges in England wore robes lined with miniver in the winter and shot pink silk in the summer, but by the mid-eighteenth century grey taffeta had replaced the pink silk. It is possible that judges in Guernsey preserved the older silk in their robes; as does the Burgon Society in its hoods.

Kit Hannah for *Bailiwick Express Guernsey*

Fig. 2. HM The King in the Channel Islands, in July 2024, accompanied by the Bailiff of Guernsey, Sir Richard McMahon.

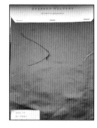

Fig. 4. Judges' ruby silk (original shade).

Fig. 1. Sir Peter Stafford Carey, Kt., Bailiff of Guernsey, by Frank Brooks (1854–1937).

Fig. 3. University of London specialist doctors' robe.

the company has supplied several of the familiar and much-admired silk and silk/rayon taffetas employed in the manufacture of academic robes.

The reference given for the ruby silk by Stephen Walters is '48 Judges' and their name for the shade of silk is 'terracotta' (Fig. 4).

Nevertheless, those present at Burgon Society gatherings cannot have failed to notice that there have, for some time, appeared to be two distinctive shades of the ruby silk used for the Congregation hoods worn by Fellows, as illustrated in the photograph in Figure 5, taken at the Congregation in the University of Chester in October 2023.

Upon investigation, it seems that a redder version of the hood had appeared around 2010, although there doesn't seem to have been any previous discussion of it. However, a meeting with James Middleton, the Academic Director of Ede & Ravenscroft Ltd, also in autumn 2023, to discuss the ruby shot silk, shed some light on the issue. It transpired that by the time the company needed a new supply of the silk, it had not been woven for several years. In the meantime, the silk weaving industry had undergone a profound change. The old shuttle looms had given way to the new automated looms and when the same crimson and ivory threads were used on them, the result was a different shade of silk. Apparently, the newer looms are more sensitive to temperature and air pressure, and both of these can affect the finished shade of the product.

Fig. 5. Two versions of the lining in the Congregation hood, seen in 2023.

Fig. 7. Prototype FBS winter hood, bound with grey possum fur.

Discussion on the ruby silk is ongoing but, for the present, the Society has decided to be relaxed about the presence of both the older and newer versions of the silks.

Currently, the Society holds a stock of FBS hoods in the more recent silk, but the archivist, occasionally, is able to recycle one of the original ruby silk hoods when it is bequeathed to it.

Meanwhile, in a curiously positive outcome to a rather tragic story, the recent demise of the academic and clerical robemaking firm of J. Wippell & Co., after almost 140 years, resulted in the Society being given a wonderful opportunity to salvage many items for the archive.[5] Amongst these, the archivist spotted a large bolt of the original judges' ruby silk, which the Society has made available to fellows and robemakers to purchase in lengths of one or two metres.[6]

Fig. 6. Ruby polyester silk substitute.

Additionally, in these days when some people reject natural fibres or prefer not to wear them, the Society has sanctioned a non-silk version of the FBS hood lining. Currently, this version of the FBS hood is available from Ede & Ravenscroft. The lining material is a flat ruby coloured fabric called Vallore, although the search continues for other alternatives (Fig. 6).

---

5 While this article was being prepared in summer 2024, news of Wippell's resurrection was announced. Watts & Co. have bought the name and will use its patterns and several of its skilled workers.

6 In order to make up a Congregation or festal hood, respectively. I'm not aware that Wippell ever made robes for Channel Islands' judges, but they did supply robes for some University of London ceremonies. Therefore, it is not surprising that they had stocked some of the ruby silk.

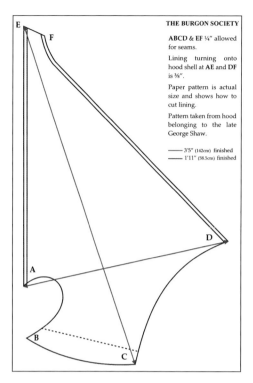

THE BURGON SOCIETY

ABCD & EF ¼" allowed for seams.

Lining turning onto hood shell at **AE** and **DF** is ⅜".

Paper pattern is actual size and shows how to cut lining.

Pattern taken from hood belonging to the late George Shaw.

—— 3'5" (142cm) finished
—— 1'11" (58.5cm) finished

E F
A
D
B
C

Fig. 8. Pattern for the Congregation hood.

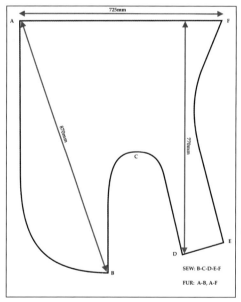

725mm
A F
870mm
770mm
C
E
B
D

SEW: B-C-D-E-F
FUR: A-B, A-F

Fig. 9 (above). Pattern for the festal hood.

Fig. 11 (right). A later festal (winter) hood, made by The Revd Kenneth Crawford, Robes of Distinction.

Chris Williams

Fig. 10. An early winter (festal) hood, made by Philip Goff from an existing corded Ottoman silk shell and using fur stripped from another hood.

Philip Goff

Fig. 12. The winter (festal) hood in Fig. 10 being shown to members of Council Colin Fleming, Prof. Bruce Christianson and Dr Nicholas Jackson, by Fr Goff, in 2009.

That other Burgon Society hood
A hood for all seasons: the festal (winter) hood;
formerly the winter (festal) hood

Seven years after the Burgon Society was founded; with several serious scholars in our midst, a growing reputation for research and the establishment of a fine and respected journal, there was, surely, time for more discussion about hoods and gowns—our raison d'être. At the Council meeting of 12 May 2007, I raised the issue of a winter hood for Fellows of the Society. Council agreed that it would welcome the sight of a 'prototype for consideration, to include fur'. The minute continues, 'Consideration needs to be given as to when it is to be worn'.[7] At the meeting I argued for use of the Warham (or medieval) shape for this hood but the mood of the Council was much more in favour of a Durham full shape.

Mention of the proposed hood appeared next in the minutes of 11 October 2008, in a single line which reads: 'Philip Goff revisited the possibility of a BS winter hood, potentially in a cosy Durham shape'.[8]

Supported by Professor Bruce Christianson, we therefore proposed to Council that, following the ancient practice in the universities of doctors wearing fur lined hoods during the winter months,[9] it sanction a hood adorned with fur as well as silk as an option for Fellows.

This 'winter hood' was agreed at a meeting of the Council on 4 July 2009, with Professor William Gibson in the chair. The minutes of the meeting record the following:

    3. Matters Arising
        d) Burgon Society Winter Hood

---

7   No. 12.

8   I am not convinced that the word 'cosy' was used but this, clearly, is what the Secretary thought he had heard.

9   Originally all university graduate hoods were lined with fur. In the early fifteenth century the practice began, at Oxford anyway, of allowing those of the rank of MA and above to substitute silk-lined hoods from Easter (moveable, but always in the spring) to All Saints' Day (1 November). For a fuller treatment of the subject of fur and silk in hoods, see Bruce Christianson et al., 'Capuciis Furruratis cum Serico Duplicatis: Furred Hoods with Silk Linings from the Late Nineteenth Century', in this volume at pp. 21–36.

A sample of a hood was presented [Fig. 7] which had been made in New Zealand:[10] modified Durham BCL shape,[11] made of black cloth, lined with ruby shot silk and bound with 2" miniver. The fur on the presented hood was possum (grey); however, as it could be bleached, there will be no prescription as to the colour used. The price was estimated at around £200. It was proposed to adopt this as the Society's winter hood, and Council passed the proposal with 6 votes in favour and 1 abstention.

In the summer 2009 issue of *Burgon Notes* a notice of the new hood appears:

At its meeting in July [2009], the Council authorised a 'winter' hood for the optional use of Fellows. The hood specification is:

> The winter hood is made in black cloth in the Society's modified Durham BCL shape, lined with crimson shot white silk,[12] and bound on cape and cowl edges with two inches of fur." By not specifying the colour of the fur (which may be real or artificial) the Society is permitting a range of fur colour to be used.

From winter to festal

It was pointed out that since the new hood was not entirely lined with fur but instead lined with the Society's ruby shot silk and bound around the cape and cowl with fur it was not, in the strict sense, a winter hood. Professor Bruce Christianson began to refer to it as a 'festal' hood and Dr Alex Kerr drily called it, 'a hood for all seasons'. The Council was clear, however, that the hood would not be worn at Congregation, the Society's annual foundation day gathering in October.[13]

Notwithstanding, the term 'festal hood' prevailed,[14] as we can see from part of an email containing information about Burgon Society dress sent by Professor Christianson to Dr Nicholas Groves, the editor of *Shaw's Academical Dress of Great Britain and Ireland*:

Academicals for Fellows.
The FBS congregation hood is of the Burgon shape [s2], in black silk, lined and bound with ruby silk (crimson shot with ivory). The FBS festal hood is of the Society's special modified Durham [f7] shape, lined with ruby silk, edged with fur inside the cowl, and bound with fur on the cape.[15] The fur may be white, with or without spots, or grey. The FBS festal hood is not worn with congregation dress.

---

10 By Paul Fielder of Étude Classique.

11 The pattern for the hood was cut on my vicarage dining room table, by Professor Bruce Christianson and Dr Nicholas Groves from a hood in the Burgon archive. It was modified somewhat by giving the liripipe a slightly wider angle.

12 As mentioned above, the warp of the silk is, in fact, off-white or ivory rather than white.

13 Council was keen to ensure that all Fellows should appear vested in similar hoods at Congregation, and the original Burgon shape hood has become known as the Congregation hood in consequence.

14 Professor Christianson points out that since several Fellows live in the opposite hemisphere of the world from the UK, the term 'winter hood' cannot adequately describe the garment.

15 Professor Christianson confesses that not only was his description inconsistent with what Council had agreed, but he had inexplicably failed to describe his own festal hood. He pleads incuria.

But the entry in Shaw reads:

> The hood is of the Durham full shape [f7], in black silk, lined with ruby shot silk, bordered inside the cowl and bound on the cape with 'miniver' (real or artificial), which may be grey, plain white or spotted ('ermine').[16]

Sorting it out

Unfortunately, the disparity in the various descriptions of the hood had led to some confusion among Fellows wishing to have a festal hood made up. Moreover, robemakers have sometimes been unsure of the precise instructions to follow (partly, because some flexibility was included in the description from the beginning). Should the hood be made from silk or cloth and does 'cloth' include silk?[17] The experience of a newish Fellow who contacted the Society for assistance, after a robemaker's unsatisfactory attempt at making up his order, prompted me to contact those others involved in the hood's creation.[18] This has led to a highly enjoyable exchange of emails among various Fellows in which we have attempted to reconcile the inconsistencies in the descriptions of the hood and to afford the Executive Committee[19] the opportunity to endorse and promulgate a definitive regulation that will assist Fellows and robemakers now and in the future.

The updated regulation

Here is the statement and approved new regulation for the Burgon Society festal hood:

> In 2009, in a nod to the ancient practice of the universities, Council introduced a second hood for fellows, adorned with fur, which may be worn on festal occasions (but not at solemn occasions such as the Society's annual Congregation). Variation of description had led to some confusion about the specification of the hood, so the Executive Committee has approved the following regulation to be followed from June 2021.
>
> The festal (or winter) hood
> A black hood of the Durham BSc shape [f7][20] lined with the Society's ruby shot silk and bound around the cape and cowl with white or grey fur, with or without spots, so that 2" fur shows all round. The fur may be real or artificial. The neckband is plain black, straight, and narrow.

Notwithstanding the above, any Fellow is entitled to wear a winter/festal hood obtained before this regulation was introduced.

The Society recognizes that Fellows may wish to have their FBS hoods made by a robemaker or tailor of their choice, or even to make them themselves. To this end, thanks to The Revd Kenneth Crawford, FBS, of Robes of Distinction, copies of the

---

16 Nicholas Groves (ed), *Shaw's Academical Dress of Great Britain and Ireland*, 3rd edn (London: Burgon Society, 2011–14), Vol. II, p. 220.

17 It does.

18 One of the robemaking companies even thought that the Society had both a winter hood and a festal hood.

19 Successor to the Council.

20 Since the Durham BCL hood is now defunct, the [f7] pattern is referred to as the Durham BSc shape in the Groves classification system. This pattern is used for all bachelors' degrees at Durham, apart from the BA and BD, but like the FBS, and unlike the BCL, the BSc has fur on the edge of the cowl, as well as on the cape.

approved patterns of both the congregation hood and festal hood are available from the Society and specimens have been deposited in our archive (Figs 8 and 9).

Whilst the Society aims for reasonable congruence in its regulation of the Congregation hood, it will be noticed that there is more scope for personal interpretation in the winter/festal, now festal/winter hood.

Afterword

Having written about the Society having two hoods, I realize that this is not strictly accurate. In fact we have three, because the original design was taken up and used in the Burgon Society logo, created by Dr John Horton, in our very early days. It depicts a dark blue [s2] hood lined and bound with crimson silk, as the Oxford MA, and surrounded by eleven Bishop Andrewes caps, representing the founders of

Fig. 13. The original Burgon Society hood appears only in the logo: dark blue bound with crimson silk, in the Burgon [s2] shape, surrounded by Bp Andrewes caps [h4].

the Society. The hood was much admired and supported but not adopted because of its similarity to the aforementioned garment. The colours, of course, have survived in the robes of our senior officers but, alas, the hood, apart from being seen in our logo, exists only as a cherished idea: perhaps as the Platonic form of the hood!

Transactions of the Burgon Society, 23 (2023), pages 23–38

Capuciis Furruratis cum Serico Duplicatis: Furred Hoods with Silk Linings from the Late Nineteenth Century

By Bruce Christianson, Philip Goff, and Nicholas Groves[†]

On 14 March 1879, Kate Milligan Edger became the first woman in the British Empire entitled to wear an academic hood trimmed with fur.[1] The hood in question, a BA from the relatively new University of New Zealand, was a black Cambridge full shape [f1], lined with pink silk (denoting Arts) and bordered with white fur (denoting a bachelor's degree).

Even twenty years previously, such a composite hood would have been a solecism:[2] for hundreds of years, hoods for graduates of British universities had been lined with either silk or fur, but not with both at once. But, by the end of the nineteenth century, the novel confluence of black hood with a coloured silk lining and a fur border had become entirely respectable,[3] to the point where some universities with established systems of academic dress retrofitted fur to their bachelors' hoods.

Fig. 1. Kate Milligan Edger, BA New Zealand, 1877.

[†] Deceased.

1   Fig. 1. Kate Edger graduated in July 1877, then had to wait nearly two years for the University to establish its system of academic dress. For a key to the Groves classification of hood patterns, see Groves, *Shaw*, Vol. I, pp. 32–39; also available at <burgon.org.uk/academic-dress/classification>. Grace Annie Lockhart graduated Bachelor of Science from Mount Allison in Canada in 1875, but Mount Allison has never used fur on its hoods. Strikingly, she wears no academic dress in her graduation class photograph, nor are any of her male classmates hooded; Fig. 2: <mta.ca/about/news/grace-annie-lockhart-mount-allison-and-canadian-heroine-mon-05172021-1708> [all web pages in this article were retrieved 14 July 2024].

In contrast, both Elena Piscopia, PhD in Letters, Padua 1678 (Fig. 3), and Laura Bassi, PhD in Science, Bologna 1732 (Fig. 4), are depicted in their official portraits wearing fur-lined doctors' capes: <en.wikipedia.org/wiki/Elena_Cornaro_Piscopia#> and <en.wikipedia.org/wiki/Laura_Bassi#>.

2   In this article, we use the term composite to refer to a hood lined with silk of a colour different from the outer, and trimmed with fur. We are particularly, but not exclusively, concerned with hoods that have black outers.

3   Although the new fashion would prove still controversial at Cambridge as late as the 1930s, as we shall see.

Fig. 2. Grace Annie Lockhart (in mufti), BSc Mount Allison, 1875.

Fig. 3. Elena Lucrezia Cornaro Piscopia, PhD (Letters) Padua, 1678.

Once, all graduates were prescribed academic hoods lined with fur

In England during the fourteenth century, the hoods of Bachelors of Arts and bachelors in the lay faculties were lined with cheap fur, such as lambswool; expensive fur, such as miniver, was used to line the hoods of the more senior degrees: doctors, Masters of Arts, and bachelors in the clerical faculties of Divinity and Canon Law.[4]

Silk linings emerge in the fifteenth century

Beginning in the fifteenth century, silk linings were introduced into the academic hoods of the senior degrees for use during the summer (officially between Easter and All Saints) as a cooler alternative to the expensive fur.[5] Bachelors (other than those in Divinity and Canon Law) were still required to line their hoods with cheap fur throughout the year.

Although the 1443 foundation statutes of All Souls College, Oxford, tantalizingly require graduate fellows to wear 'furred hoods lined with silk according to their degrees',[6] it is not clear whether this refers to an early appearance of the combination lining of silk and fur that would (re)-emerge during the latter part of the nineteenth century, or the Latin formula is simply a convenient way of referring to both types of hood.

---

4   The lay faculties were Civil Law, Medicine, and (later) Music. The clerical bachelors' degrees in Divinity and Canon Law typically required the same length of study as the lay doctorates; the clerical doctorates took twice this long.

5   Silk linings were permitted as a summer alternative at Bologna as early as 1410, and Oxford followed shortly thereafter, although Cambridge waited nearly 150 years before granting her masters and doctors general permission: see Hargreaves-Mawdsley, *Academical Dress*; and Christianson, 'Oxford Blues', for more details.

6   'Omnesque et singuli Socii graduati, cum superpellitiis suis hujusmodi, utantur capuciis furruratis , cum serico duplicatis, suis gradibus congruentibus.' See Bond, Vol. I, 'Statutes of All Souls College, Oxford', p. 47; Groves, 'Quire'. Our thanks to Dr Alex Kerr for his comments. The search for an irrefutable instance of a medieval composite hood continues.

Fig. 4 (left).
Laura Maria
Caterina Bassi,
PhD (Science)
Bologna,
1732.

Fig. 5 (right).
John Bull,
BMus Oxford,
1586.

In any event, at some point, although it is not clear exactly when, the divines, lay doctors, and Masters of Arts at the English universities ceased to change back into their fur hoods for winter,[7] and a silk (rather than fur) lining became the year-round marker of a senior degree.

The Oxford BCL becomes an exception

Most academic hoods were made of the same material as the gown or habit over which they were worn, which in the English universities was, by the fifteenth century, typically black stuff for Bachelors of Arts, black silk for Masters of Arts, and scarlet cloth for doctors.

But somehow, by the end of the sixteenth century, the lay bachelors at Oxford (Bachelors of Civil Law, Medicine, and Music) were wearing a hood made entirely of blue silk, lined with cheap fur.[8] Scandalously, this simple-shaped blue hood was increasingly merely trimmed with fur, rather than fully lined as the rules required and, by the time of Grignion in 1770, the proctors appear to have given up the battle.[9]

Although these hoods are made entirely of coloured silk, rather than lined with it, they represent a half-way house to the composite hoods that were to emerge later.

7   Although there are some interesting survivals. At Oxford the proctors still wear the miniver-lined winter version of the MA hood—but they do so all year round; at Cambridge in 1815 Ackermann depicts lay doctors still wearing fur-lined hoods with their congregation robes regardless of the season; Jackson, Plates XIV (Oxford), IV (Cambridge). In contrast, High Court judges in England continued to change their robes twice a year until 2008: their robes were faced with miniver until Ascension Day, and then with pink shot silk until 28 October.

8   The evolution of the Oxford lay bachelors' hoods is discussed in more detail in Christianson, 'Evolution'. In the wonderful 1589 portrait of John Bull, BMus, Fig. 5, his blue silk hood is damask and the fur looks decidedly expensive, but Oxford musicians have a reputation as free spirits when it comes to academic dress: <en.wikipedia.org/wiki/John_Bull_(composer)>.

9   Hargreaves-Mawdsley, *Academical Dress*, Plates 11 B and C. (Grignion was the engraver of a set of plates.)

A medical false-hood

Hargreaves-Mawdsley refers to a 1651 portrait of Sir Charles Scarburgh, MD, as depicting him wearing 'a very large white fur hood with only a thin line of pink silk showing', which would seem to describe an early example of the type of composite hood we are considering.[10]

However, Kerr briskly dispels this figment: 'The thin strip about an inch wide between the fur covering above and the fur binding below is not pink silk but scarlet cloth, exactly the same colour as Scarburgh's Convocation habit: it is part of the shell of the hood and not some silk facing. These hoods, like the habits, could still be lined with either fur or silk (but surely not both together).'[11]

A legal fiction

Hargreaves-Mawdsley also describes in similar terms a 'scarlet cloth hood lined with scarlet taffeta and edged with miniver' as being worn by members of Doctors' Commons serving as advocates in the Court of Arches,[12] but his sources all lead eventually back to Strype who actually says:

> Advocates are such as have taken their Degree of Doctor in the Faculty of the Civil Law; or (when this Kingdom submitted to the Papal See) of the Canon Law … The Habits they use in Court, both Judges and Advocates, are a Scarlet Robe, and a Hood lined with Taffata, if they be of Oxford; if of Cambridge, White Minever, and round Caps of Black Velvet.[13]

This seems to describe conventional academic hoods worn at the time by Doctors of Law.

Durham introduces two-tone silk hoods trimmed with fur

In March 1858, Gutch refers to the hood for the Bachelor of Medicine at Durham as 'purple cloth bound with white fur', but this appears to have been premature:[14] his revised list for September of that year replaces this description with 'not decided upon by the Senatus'.

In October 1863, the *Lancet* describes the MB as 'palatinate purple silk, lined with scarlet edged with ermine'.[15] Their source for this assertion is unclear, and the reference to ermine is intriguing, albeit historically inappropriate for a Bachelor of Medicine. Wood's description in 1875, 'Scarlet silk, lined with palatinate purple silk, and bound with white fur', places the colours the opposite (i.e., correct) way around, but confirms the precedent: silk of two different colours, one of them a lining, and the result trimmed with fur.[16]

---

10 Op. cit., p. 76, n. 3. The picture is reproduced here: <digitalcollections.nyam.org /islandora/object/ladd%253A241>.

11 Kerr, pp. 119–20.

12 *Legal Dress*, p. 94.

13 Strype, Book I, Chapter 24, p. 155.

14 The first MB was awarded in 1858. The Durham BCL did end up being palatinate purple silk, bound with white fur, which may have been inspired partly by the Oxford model, but the Durham BCL hood, like the MB and the later BSc, has always been full.

15 Vol. 82, p. 406. The *Lancet* probably had their MB hood on back to front.

16 Fig. 6, for which our gratitude to Dr Giles Brightwell. Newcastle took this hood with

Fig. 6 (left). Durham MB.

Fig 7 (right). LLB Edinburgh, post 1866.

Lee Dobson

Burgon Society Archive WGC-122

Wood (in 1875 and in 1882) refers to the Durham MusB as 'White silk, lined with palatinate purple silk, and bound with fur', which follows the same model as the MB. However, this specification did not survive: Fowler in 1904 states the regulations for the Durham MusB hood as 'Palatinate purple silk, bound with brocaded white satin',[17] as do the subsequent sources, and Haycraft in 1923 specifies that the MusB hood is by then simple shape.

---

them when they departed in 1963. On the modern Newcastle MB the hood is [f7] and only the cape has fur, and this was probably the Durham practice for it from the beginning, with Medicine conforming to Law in this respect, rather than to Science, which has fur on both cape and cowl. Later composite hoods at Durham that followed the model of the MB include the BCom, black lined cerise, cape bound fur, which dates from 1917; and the BDS, rose lined ivory, cape bound fur, first awarded 1932, which also went with Newcastle.

17 Fowler, Appendix VIII. The MusB had been awarded *ad eundem* to graduates of Oxford, Cambridge, and Dublin since 1863, but the first MusB by examination was not until 1891. The 1890 calendar agrees with Wood, whereas that for 1892 gives the BMus the BCL hood. Our thanks to Dr Paul Coxon for assistance with the Durham sources, and for many helpful comments.

Fig. 8. Helen Connan, BA New Zealand, 1880.

Fig. 9. University of New Zealand: left Margaret Lilian Florence Edger, BA, 1881; centre Helen Connon, MA, 1881; right Kate Milligan Edger, BA, 1877.

Edinburgh takes the next step with a simple black outer

In the University of Edinburgh calendar for 1865–66, hoods for bachelors' degrees appear for the first time.[18] The four hoods (for the LLB, BD, MB, and ScB) follow a regular system: they are made of black silk in a simple shape, lined with the faculty colour silk already used by the corresponding doctor's degree (blue, purple, crimson, and lemon yellow, respectively), and 'bordered with white fur'.

New Zealand goes the full Monty

The University of New Zealand was founded in 1870, but did not prescribe a system of hoods until 1879. All hoods were the 'same size and shape as that of the Cambridge Master of Arts', lined with coloured silk denoting the faculty: the first two faculty colours to be specified were pink for Arts, and pale blue for Law.[19] In addition to the lin-

18 For details of this development see Cooper, p. 125. These Edinburgh bachelors' hoods were and still are [s4]; Fig. 7. In this paper, we use the term 'faculty colour' in the same sense as Christianson, 'Gold', p. 80, n. 1.

19 In 1879 pink was for boys, and pale blue was for girls; see Bilal. The black outers were initially made of silk, as at Cambridge, although this was never specified in the regulations. The first academic dress regulations were agreed by the Senate on 14 March 1879; the first mention in the press of a hood being conferred on a graduand during the course of a degree ceremony was the 6 August following. The regulations required all graduates to 'appear at all public ceremonials of the University [which included graduation] in the academical costume

ing, the bachelors' hoods were 'bordered with white fur':[20] making these the first black full-shape composite hoods for a university degree.

But was Chichester Theological College there first?

In 1882, the bishops of the Church of England regulated the linings of the English theological college hoods. Prior to this restriction, Chichester used a black Cambridge full shape hood, lined with violet silk and bound on all edges with white fur.[21] It is not clear when this hood was adopted: Chichester did not accept non-graduates prior to 1846, so the hood is unlikely to pre-date this, but it is at least possible that it was deployed before the composite bachelors' hoods at Durham and Edinburgh, and very likely that it pre-dates the black full hoods at New Zealand.

Ironically, if this is the case, the combination of silk lining and fur trim may have been chosen to ensure the hood did not resemble that for a university degree, following which the hood was suppressed by the bishops because fashion had changed, and now it did.

St Andrews briefly mirrors Durham

St Andrews added a white fur trimming to the cowl of its bachelors' hoods in 1888.[22] For twenty years prior to this, bachelors had worn the hood of a doctor in the same faculty. The doctors' hoods were already lined with white satin, intended to represent the pre-Reformation miniver, and so for a short period the bachelors had a hood in faculty colour silk, lined with white satin (representing expensive fur) and trimmed with cheap fur. Eventually the situation was regularized and the white satin lining was removed,[23] leaving the bachelors' hoods as they are today.

---

proper to their degree', so some in the audience were already hooded, including (as it happens) Kate Edger: <www.canterbury.ac.nz/about-uc/what-we-do/uc-in-the-community/exhibitions-and-collections/canterbury-college/open-doors/graduation-and-celebrations> (seated centre). The first woman to be hooded during a ceremony was Helen Connan, who took her BA on 30 July 1880; Fig. 8.

20 At the time, Cambridge cut the BA and MA in slightly different shapes, but the New Zealand system was designed so that a BA hood could be converted to MA simply by removing the fur border. A year after her BA, Helen Connan became the first woman in the British Empire to be admitted to the degree of MA, at Canterbury University College on 15 August 1881: Fig. 9, seated centre. Standing on Helen's left is Kate Edger, wearing her fur-trimmed BA hood; on her right is Kate's younger sister Lilian, who graduated BA in 1881 at the same ceremony. Kate and Lilian would graduate MA together at Canterbury the following year. It thus appears that New Zealand bachelors' hoods originally had fur trim on the edge of the cape as well as the cowl, as evidenced by Helen Connan and Lilian Edger with their BA hoods in Figs 8 and 9, respectively.

21 See Groves, *Shaw*, Vol. II, p. 103; Groves, *Theological Colleges*; Wood 1882. Wood 1875 makes no mention at all of Chichester.

22 Cooper, p. 135, and Fig. 11, p. 134.

23 It is not clear exactly when, but the satin was gone by the time of Ealand in 1920. A new composite hood was approved much later at St Andrews for the EdB: black, lined primrose, bound fur; this degree went with Dundee when they gained their independence in 1967, although they gave it a new hood.

The new fashion spreads (but only a little) to 19th-century USA

Bryn Mawr is an historically women's college in Pennsylvania, founded in 1885, ten years before the Intercollegiate Code was established in the USA. Bryn Mawr would modify the code, by trimming their black BA hood with white fur in place of white velvet. The silk lining is old gold with a white chevron.

The University of the South, Tennessee (founded 1857), is listed in Wood 1882 as having one composite hood, for its BCL: a black simple hood, lined green and edged with white fur, but it not clear when this hood was first worn, or indeed if it ever was. Chitty asserts that at the July 1872 meeting of the trustees, designs for the hoods of twelve degrees were approved 'in the same designs and colours [still being] used in 1952',[24] but by the time of Haycraft 1923 the fur has been replaced in the specification by a purple cord.

Lincoln-Jefferson University in Chicago, founded 1897, has for its BA in Haycraft a black hood, lined purple and edged with white fur. This institution was a notorious degree mill, which included Charles Franklyn among its 'graduates'.[25]

Manchester retrofits fur

In April 1901, the Council of the Victoria University of Manchester approved the addition of the words 'with a white fur lining inside the edging' to the description of the hoods for the BA and BSc degrees.[26] The linings of fur and silk are thus placed the opposite way around to most hoods of the composite type.

The change met with general approval, according to the *Owens College Union Magazine*, which referred to it as 'a change ... which will not appeal to lady students only', and subsequently to 'the general popularity of the becoming change which has so much relieved the dullness of the Bachelors' hoods ...'[27]

Liverpool adopted a variant of the Edinburgh system when it left the Victoria University in 1903, which incorporated black composite hoods for bachelors' degrees.[28]

More Colonial universities embrace the trend

In 1894 Melbourne University replaced their BSc hood with a composite: black simple shape, lined moss green silk and edged with white fur. In 1902 the University instigated a system of faculty colour linings, and prescribed composite hoods for all bachelors.[29]

The University of Western Australia, founded in Perth in 1911, adopted composite hoods for all its bachelors' degrees: black simple shape, lined with watered silk of the faculty colour and edged with white fur. The first faculty colours were royal blue for Arts; emerald green for Science; gold for Engineering; royal purple for Law; peacock blue for Music; and ruby red for Medicine.

---

24 The first degrees were awarded at the University of the South in August 1874, but this cohort included no BCLs; Chitty, pp. 138, 182, n. 7.

25 Groves, *Charles Franklyn*, pp. 30–32. All LJU hoods are said to be full by Haycraft, but Franklyn's hood in Groves, op. cit., Fig. 2, p. 32, is clearly the Burgon shape.

26 Figure 10. The original design without fur had been approved twenty years earlier.

27 Lowe, pp. 17, 8.

28 Fig. 11.

29 University of Melbourne Calendars, 1858–2009, at <umpc.esrc.unimelb.edu.au/biogs /E000008b.htm>. The fur edgings were replaced with white silk bindings in 1927.

Fig. 10. BA Manchester, post 1901.

Fig. 11. BA Liverpool.

Fig. 12. BA Dalhousie.

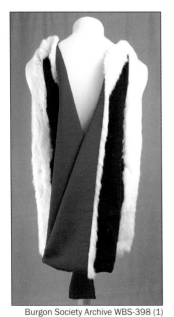

Fig. 13. BCom McGill.

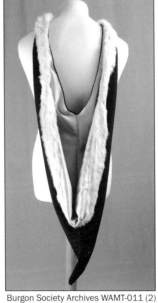

Fig. 14. Fellow of the National College of Music.

Fig. 15. Fellow of the Victoria College of Music.

During the period between 1889 and 1923, a number of Canadian universities also adopted composite hoods for at least one of their bachelors' degrees. Here are some examples, all are simple shape except where indicated:

> King's College Halifax: BSc—black, lined old gold,[30] edged white fur.
>
> New Brunswick: BSc (Arts)—black, lined scarlet, bordered white fur; similarly BSc (Applied), lined green.
>
> Dalhousie: BA—black, lined white, bordered fur.[31]
>
> McGill[32] (full shape with fur edging outside both cowl and cape): BA—black, lined pale blue, edged white fur; similarly BCL, French grey; BArch, white; BSc, yellow; BMus, mauve.
>
> Manitoba: Bachelor of Civil Engineering—black, lined yellow, edged white fur; similarly Bachelor of Pharmacy, lined light blue.
>
> Bishop's University Lennoxville (full): BA—black, lined violet, bordered white fur.[33]
>
> McMaster University, Toronto: BA—black, lined white silk, edged white fur.
>
> Victoria University Toronto:[34] (full) BD—black, lined purple, trimmed ermine [!]

Non-university hoods: English music colleges (all simple shape)

We have already mentioned that Chichester Theological College prescribed a composite hood until it was forbidden by the bishops. Composite hoods were also prescribed for non-degree qualifications by a number of the English music colleges, which were not subject to episcopal oversight.

Trinity College of Music at some point between 1872 and 1875[35] prescribed for its Senior Choral Fellows a black hood in a simple shape, lined with violet silk and bound with white fur. By 1882 this had become the hood for a Licentiate in Music, with the Licentiate in Arts having a pink lining in place of the violet one.

The Guild of Organists, founded 1887, gave their fellows a black hood, lined rose pink[36] and faced 6" fur. By the time of Haycraft 1923 a number of other music colleges had followed this example:

> Incorporated Guild of Church Musicians: Life Fellows—crimson, lined gold shot,[37] bound fur.

---

30 There was also, briefly, a BEng on the same pattern with a green lining.

31 Fig. 12.

32 Fig. 13. Wood 1882 sets out a very different system, without composite hoods or faculty colours. The new system was in place by 1903.

33 The specification is virtually the same as Chichester; since 1906 a very similar hood adorned a New Zealand Bachelor of Engineering. These congruences were observed by Baty.

34 Listed in Ealand, p. 311. The ermine did not last long, but the hood has probably always been full.

35 The exact dates are not known, because the relevant records were destroyed in the Blitz: Groves, *Shaw*, Vol. I, pp. 94–96; Groves and Kersey; however, the violet hood is described in Wood 1875 as the hood for a Senior Choral Fellow; and both composite hoods are listed, as licentiate hoods, in Wood 1882.

36 Wood 1889 has this lining as rose pink; by the time of Haycraft 1923 the lining is given as crimson, possibly to avoid confusion with the LTCM (Arts).

37 The gold lining was added to the original crimson hood at some point prior to 1923.

National Academy of Music, c. 1920: Fellow—navy blue, lined red, bound fur.[38]

National College of Music, 1894: Fellow—black, lined lavender, bound fur on cowl.[39]

Victoria College of Music, 1890: Fellow—royal blue, lined scarlet, cowl bordered with white fur.[40]

Another non-university institution to adopt a composite hood for their fellowship, albeit in the full shape, is the Burgon Society, to whose festal hood we turn after the following interlude.

A bridge too far: the Cambridge reforms of 1934

In 1934 Cambridge University established a system of faculty colours for its hoods, by extending the use of the silks distinctive of the various doctors' degrees[41] to lower degrees in the same faculty.

The 1934 reforms were the culmination of a series of consultations that had taken place over the previous two years.[42] The first (1932) report of the Council to the Senate proposed that masters in the lay faculties should have a black hood lined inside with faculty-colour silk; and bachelors the same, but trimmed on the cape with white fur, i.e., exactly the type of composite hood we have been considering.

In between the first (1932) and second (1933) reports of the Council to the Senate, the faculty-coloured silk proposed for bachelors' degrees moved from being an inside lining to forming the entire body of the hood, as it does now, and a fur facing was added to the cowl edge. This was purportedly to bring the other bachelors' hoods into line with the Cambridge MusB hood;[43] the first proposal may have savoured more of nineteenth-century novelty.[44]

Cambridge adopts a composite hood anyway

All was not lost for the 1932 proposal, however. The Cambridge degree of BEd, first awarded in 1969, had a black outer with a blue silk lining, and was faced on the cowl edge and bound on the cape with white fur.[45]

---

38 Compare this with the Victoria College of Music below.

39 Fig. 14; Groves and Kersey, Plate 4.

40 Fig. 15.

41 The systematic use of distinctive colours for doctorates in different faculties was itself an innovation dating from the reforms of 1889; Groves, 'Cambridge'. For a long time prior to this date, bachelors and masters in all faculties at Cambridge had worn a hood reflecting their status in the Faculty of Arts.

42 The various reports are to be found in Franklyn, along with Franklyn's irascible commentary.

43 Which itself dated only from 1889, and was described without apparent irony by Council in their second report as 'perhaps the most beautiful of all academic decorations'; Franklyn, p. 183. To be fair to Cambridge, their new MusB hood did have some precedent in the older Durham BCL, whereas the 1932 proposals followed the 1917 Durham BCom.

44 Although so also were the faculty-specific silks for doctors, and indeed faculty hood schemes generally.

45 Fig. 16: our thanks to Ryder & Amies for the loan of this hood. The degree is no longer awarded.

Decline and fall

New systems that included composite hoods continued to be defined,[46] but by the 1960s, enthusiasm for composite hoods and indeed for fur generally was on the wane in the university sector.

Strathclyde in 1964 used fur as the faculty 'colour' for Engineering; Stirling and the Royal College of Art adopted composite hoods in 1967, but not for their bachelors: both adopted fur for masters' degrees, and the RCA for higher doctors as well;[47] Dundee in 1967 adopted composite hoods for their bachelors;[48] Brandon in 1967[49] adopted a composite hood for their BSc; and Saskatchewan flirted with a composite hood for their BA (PhysEd).[50]

Composite non-university hoods of relatively recent vintage include the Fellowship of the North and Midlands School of Music;[51] the Institute of Traditional Anglicans;[52] the Llandaff Diocese Ordination Course;[53] and of course ...

The Burgon Society festal hood

The Burgon Society was founded to combine study of the design, history and practice of academic dress, and so Council (as the Executive Committee was then called) decided in 2009 that it would be fun to adopt a second official Society hood for festive occasions,[54] along the lines of the nineteenth-century composite hoods that we have been considering in this article.

Following a fruitful period of experimentation, the specification for this hood has settled down, and is now as follows:

> A black hood of the Durham BSc shape [f7], lined with the Society's ruby shot silk and bound around the cape and cowl with white or grey fur, with or without spots, so that 2" fur shows all round. The fur may be real or artificial. The neckband is plain black, straight, and narrow.

Although partly inspired by the 'furruratis cum serico duplicatis' clause of the All Souls College Statute, this hood is not, strictly speaking, a 'winter' hood at all: Dr Alex Kerr refers to it drily as 'a hood for all seasons', which is very appropriate for a society with members in both hemispheres.

Our final figures show two examples of a Burgon festal hood,[55] together with a contemporary BA hood from the University of Auckland for comparison.[56]

---

46 This article makes no attempt to give a systematic account of developments within the last hundred years, but see Groves, *Key*; and Smith, Vol. III.

47 See Fleming for details of Stirling.

48 Fig. 17. The hoods are [a6]. The fur is removed to make the corresponding master's degree.

49 When they separated from McMaster. The hood is [f1], ochre, lined light blue, edged, fur.

50 Simple, black, lined gold, bordered fur.

51 Originally [f1] black, lined and bound 2" red satin, cowl faced 3" fur.

52 Black [s2], lined crimson, cowl bound 1" fur each side.

53 Black [f1], lined dark blue, cowl faced 3" fur, with 1" old gold set 1" in; Fig. 18.

54 This hood was designed by the authors, and the full story of the process is told in this volume; see Goff.

55 Fig. 19 is Professor William Gibson's festal hood, made by the Revd Kenneth Crawford (Robes of Distinction); the fur is faux ermine. Fig. 20 is Professor Bruce Christianson's festal hood, made by Paul Fielder, FBS (Étude Classique); the fur is unbleached grey possum (see Appendix).

56 Fig. 21. This hood is also from Étude Classique; the fur is bleached possum. Auckland

Fig. 16. BEd Cambridge.

Fig. 17. BSc Dundee.

Fig. 18. Llandaff Diocese Ordination Course.

Fig. 19. Fellow of the Burgon Society, festal hood with faux ermine.

Fig. 20. Fellow of the Burgon Society, festal hood with natural grey possum fur.

Fig. 21. BA Auckland, with bleached white possum fur.

Conclusion

Composite hoods, 'furred and lined with silk', remain in use at many institutions, but they have not for some time featured regularly in new systems of academic dress. As demand increased for cruelty-free alternatives to traditional materials, synthetic substitutes for silk became popular with academic robe designers[57] but, for whatever reasons, the synthetic substitutes for fur have not.[58]

Even Liverpool, which adopted a variant of the Edinburgh system when it left the Victoria University in 1903, has not extended the use of fur to recently introduced bachelors' degrees, and none of the post-1992 developments in the UK has embraced it. This article therefore charts not only the rise—but perhaps also the fall—of an academic dress tradition.

References

Baty, Thomas, *Academic Colours* (Tokyo: Kenkyusha Press, 1934).

Bilal, Khadia, 'Pink for Boys and Blue for Girls', *The Vintage Magazine*, May 2019, at <www.thevintagenews.com/2019/05/01/pink-blue/>.

Bond, Edward Augustus, *Statutes of the Colleges of Oxford: With Royal Patents of Foundation, Injunctions of Visitors, and Catalogues of Documents Relating to the University, Preserved in the Public Record Office* (Oxford, 1853), Vol. I.

Chitty, Arthur Benjamin, Jr, *Reconstruction at Sewanee: The Founding of the University of the South and its First Administration, 1857–1872* (Sewanee, Tennessee: The University Press, 1954).

Christianson, Bruce, 'The Evolution of the Oxford Simple Shape', *Burgon Society Annual 2002*, pp. 30–36.

Christianson, Bruce, 'Oxford Blues: The Search for the Origins of the Lay Bachelors' Hood', *Burgon Society Annual 2003*, pp. 24–28.

Christianson, Bruce, 'Lined with Gold: London University and the Colour of Science', *TBS*, 5 (2005), pp. 80–89.

Cooper, Jonathan C., 'Reforms to Scottish Academical Dress during the 1860s', *TBS*, 19 (2019), pp. 122–51.

Cox, Noel, 'Academical Dress in New Zealand', at <www.geocities.ws/noelcox/Introduction.htm>.

Ealand, Charles Aubrey (ed.), *Athena: A Year-book of the Learned World—the English-Speaking Nations* (London: A. & C. Black, 1920) Vol. I [no more published].

Fleming, Colin A. M., *Malachite and Silver: Academic Dress of the University of Stirling* (London: Burgon Society, 2009).

University College became a university in its own right when the federal University of New Zealand was dissolved in 1961, and inherited its academic dress. Nothing about the BA has changed officially from the time of Kate Edger: indeed, when Kate's granddaughter Jill Smith took her BA from Auckland University in 1985 she wore Kate's hood, with the fur trim restored. The pink on the modern hood is perhaps slightly lighter; the fur trim is confined to the cowl; at some point prior to the 1970s the outer has shifted from black silk to black cloth; and more recently the cape has become slightly rounded. In contrast, when Canterbury University College became a university, they abandoned the use of fur altogether. Our thanks to the Revd Dr Noel Cox for his assistance with New Zealand academic dress.

57 And with young people.

58 The recent MFA at TCD is an exception, although (like the Oxford BCL) it is not actually a composite hood.

Fowler, Joseph Thomas, *Durham University: Earlier Foundations and Present Colleges* (London: F. E. Robinson & Co., 1904).

Franklyn, Charles A. H., *Academical Dress from the Middle Ages to the Present Day, Including Lambeth Degrees* (Lewes: privately printed by W. E. Baxter, 1970).

Goff, Philip, 'The Development of the Burgon Society Hoods', *TBS*, 23 (2023), pp. 15–22.

Groves, Nicholas, *Theological Colleges: Their Hoods and Histories* (London: Burgon Society, 2004).

Groves, Nicholas, 'The Use of the Academic Hood in Quire', *TBS*, 8 (2008), pp. 98–105.

Groves, Nicholas, *Key to the Identification of Academic Hoods of the British Isles*, 4th edn (London: Burgon Society, 2010).

Groves, Nicholas, *Charles Franklyn: A Man of Strong Opinions* (London: Burgon Society, 2023).

Groves, Nicholas, assisted by Paul Coxon and John Horton, 'The Academic Robes of Graduates of the University of Cambridge from the End of the Eighteenth Century to the Present Day', *TBS*, 13 (2013), pp. 74–100.

Groves, Nicholas, and Kersey, John, *Academical Dress of Music Colleges and Societies of Musicians in the United Kingdom, with Notes on Degrees and Diplomas in Music of Certain Other Institutions* (London: Burgon Society, 2002).

Groves, Nicholas (ed.), *Shaw's Academical Dress of Great Britain and Ireland*, 3rd edn (London: The Burgon Society, 2011–14), 2 vols. Vol. I: *Universities and Other Degree-Awarding Bodies* (2011). Vol. II: *Non-Degree-Awarding Bodies* (2014).

Gutch, J. W. G., 'University Hoods', *Notes & Queries*, 2nd ser., 5 (1858), p. 402; 6 (1858) pp. 211–12.

Hargreaves-Mawdsley, W. N., *A History of Academical Dress in Europe until the End of the Eighteenth Century* (Oxford: Clarendon Press, 1963; reprinted Westport Conn.: Greenwood Press, 1978).

Hargreaves-Mawdsley, W. N., *A History of Legal Dress in Europe until the End of the Eighteenth Century* (Oxford: Clarendon Press, 1963).

Haycraft, Frank W., *The Degrees and Hoods of the World's Universities and Colleges*, 1st edn (Ware, Herts.: privately printed by Jennings & Bewley, 1923).

Haycraft, Frank W., *The Degrees and Hoods of the World's Universities and Colleges*, 2nd edn (London and Cheshunt: privately printed by Cheshunt Press, 1924).

Haycraft, Frank W., *The Degrees and Hoods of the World's Universities and Colleges*, 3rd edn (London and Cheshunt: privately printed by Cheshunt Press, 1927).

Jackson, Nicholas (ed.), *Ackermann's Costumes of the Universities of Oxford and Cambridge*, Burgon Society Historical Reprints, 1 (London: Burgon Society, 2016).

Kerr, Alex, 'Hargreaves-Mawdsley's *History of Academical Dress* and the Pictorial Evidence for Great Britain and Ireland: Notes and Corrections', *TBS*, 8 (2008), pp. 106–50.

Lowe, Philip, *Manchester Academic Dress: The Origins and Development of Academical Dress at the Victoria University of Manchester, 1880 to the Present Day* (Manchester: the author, 2002).

Smith, Hugh, assisted by Kevin Sheard, *Academic Dress and Insignia of the World*, 3 vols (Cape Town: A. A. Balkema, 1970).

Strype, John, *A Survey of the Cities of London and Westminster* (London, 1720).

Wood, Thomas William, *Ecclesiastical and Academical Colours* (London and Derby: Bemrose & Sons, [1875]).

Wood, Thomas William, *The Degrees, Gowns and Hoods of the British, Colonial, Indian and American Universities and Colleges* (London: Thomas Pratt & Co. [1882]; reissued with four pages of corrections and additions [*c.* 1889]).

Appendix: A brief note on the use of possum fur in New Zealand

The Australian brushtail possum (*trichosurus vulpecula*), a cat-sized marsupial, was introduced to New Zealand in 1837 for the fur trade in a horrible error of judgement.[59] In Australia, the possum is protected as a native species. But in New Zealand, it has become the country's most damaging animal pest, wreaking havoc on native flora and fauna, increasing carbon emissions while driving endemic species towards extinction, and acting as a vector of bovine tuberculosis.[60]

It is a pity, as possums are cute and good pets, but New Zealand's conservation policy towards possums continues to be extermination.[61] While this is proceeding, the fur of culled possums is widely used (in bleached form) to trim the bachelors' hoods of the four universities in New Zealand that still prescribe fur borders for them. The natural colour of the possum's coat in New Zealand is either black or grey.

---

59 <teara.govt.nz/en/possums/page-1>

60 <nzpocketguide.com/new-zealand-hates-possums/>

61 <www.doc.govt.nz/globalassets/documents/science-and-technical/possumcontrol.pdf>, <www.scientificamerican.com/article/behind-new-zealands-wild-plan-to-purge-all-pests1/>.

Transactions of the Burgon Society, 23 (2023), pages 39–74

Designing in Circles, Conversing in Triangles, Dressing in Squares: Evolving the Academic Dress of the University of Sussex, 1958–1963

By Andrew Plant

Abstract and methodology

The University of Sussex was the first of seven Plateglass Universities[1] created in England during a major expansion of higher education following the Second World War.[2] Paradoxically, the determined modernist outlook of the foundation led to a reimagining of some of the oldest elements of academic costume. With this unorthodoxy came startling departures from the parameters then obtaining, notably an unmistakable bachelors' hood with a lining of grey fur squares, the allocation of a *pileus* for officials and holders of higher doctorates, and the discarding of scarlet or claret robes in favour of innovative designs in vivid shades of yellow. This eccentricity attracted opprobrium, speculation, bewilderment, and several urban myths, although its indebtedness to older models was frequently asserted. Influences on Hargreaves-Mawdsley's original scheme are here posited and discussed for the first time, especially his unique reinterpretation of heraldic furs, and the iconographic medieval glass in the Chapel of Merton College, Oxford.

This complex gestation and development is explored through unpublished material held at the extensive archives of The Keep, Brighton, including many rare examples of animated correspondence in the notoriously challenging handwriting of Charles Franklyn. These have been deciphered as far as possible, and the majority presented in full.

For reasons of space, what follows here is only the first chapter of a longer study.

Preliminary negotiations for a university in Brighton had begun in 1911, but it would not be until February 1957 that matters gained real momentum, prompted by a debate on higher education in the House of Lords. Progress towards the new foundation was keenly observed by Charles Franklyn, who had long desired the potential pearl of Sussex, and he alerted William Stone, Director of Education for the County Borough of Brighton, to his services in customary unbridled fashion. Stone would create the colleges of further education that amalgamated into Brighton Polytechnic, and later became the University of Brighton; but Franklyn's application to design for an insti-

---

1   A term coined by Michael Beloff in *The Plateglass Universities* (1968); in fact, the dominant feature of Sussex is red brick.

2   It was quickly followed by York (1963), Warwick (1964), East Anglia, Essex, Lancaster, and Kent at Canterbury (all 1966); in Scotland, the University of Stirling was founded in 1967.

tution before the establishment of its forerunner must be something of a record, even for him.[3]

Sunday 27 April 1958
A University College for Sussex at Brighton
Dear Mr Stone,

For years I have followed with much interest the plan for a University College, growing into a University for Sussex: we have been connected with Brighton since 1887 at least and lived in Hove 1908–12. My own connection with Universities is considerable, a member of the Standing Committee, Uni's of London since Feb 1927 & Senior member since Jan 1934 & just reselected in Jan. until 1961. If you have in your office a 'Who's Who' & 'Kelly's Handbook to the T.L. [Titled, Landed] and Official Classes' you would find ample details, the main parts being that I designed the complete systems of Academical and Official dress for 4 British Universities, most of that for a 5th (Nottingham)[4] & the new hood for Chichester Theological College in Nov. 1948. I also designed the Arms for St Peter's Hall, Oxford, Malaya University etc, and put through the Patents as also for The British Transport Commission (England & Wales & Scotland) in 1956. When a University College is established, robes will be needed for the President & Principal: a degree granting University graduate robes will be necessary. These I would like to design. If you are not the right man for me to write to, kindly tell me who is, & I will also keep in touch with Walter Oakeshott as he was head boy at my school.[5]

Yours sincerely, Charles Franklyn

Franklyn was fully aware of the standing of a University College, since the universities of Exeter, Hull, Leicester, Nottingham, Reading and Southampton had begun as such. Stone's amicable reply the next day was happily oblivious to the lengthy, obstinate, and ultimately fruitless correspondence that would be precipitated. His point that no-one was yet able to consider such matters had no effect on Franklyn, who at once dispatched a postcard with his habitual trope.

30 April 1958

Many thanks indeed for your kind letter of yesterday; let us keep in close touch. Regarding Arms, I have a basic design in mind now which might (when the time comes) form a useful starting point for consideration. Southampton & Hull have the most beautiful systems of Academical Dress in Great Britain, probably in the world.

Yours sincerely, Charles Franklyn (By the way, I am not 'Mr'!)

---

3   It is necessary only to direct the reader unhesitatingly to Groves, *Charles Franklyn: A Man of Strong Opinions* (2022).

4   Franklyn's input to Nottingham, later described as 'revise and convert' (see below) was minor, and seems to have been confined to changing the hood shape (Groves, p. 50). Much of Nottingham's system, notably partly lined hoods, with Cambridge gowns for bachelors, does not reflect his habitual practice. It is possible that the blue University silk is Franklyn's suggestion, but he certainly would not have stopped there unless constrained.

5   Walter Oakeshott (former school captain of Tonbridge) was then rector of Lincoln College Oxford and a member of the Academic Planning Committee of the Preliminary Council for the University College of Sussex. Franklyn must have discovered his involvement, although the implication that Oakeshott would discuss such presumably confidential matters with him reads like an unsubtle attempt to pull strings.

The official announcement of John Fulton[6] as the new vice-chancellor spurred Franklyn to try again.

Sat 21 Feb 1959

Dear Mr Stone,

Further to your kind letter of 28th last,[7] I was most interested to learn from today's Times p. 4 of the advances made and of the nomination of the first V-C of U.C. of Sussex, Normally, a U.C. has a Principal, & he becomes usually the 1st V-C when full University status is attained.

Having designed the complete systems of academical and official dress for four British Universities (see 'Who's Who' etc), having given to Southampton and Hull the most beautiful systems (surpassing Oxford, Cambridge and London) and having been associated with Sussex since 1887 at least, I would very naturally love to give to the University in Sussex an equally fine beautiful system. The PhD Southampton has been admired continuously since its creation.

On the arms side, I designed the Arms for St Peter's Hall, Oxford, Canford School, Malaya, and the British Transport Commission, Bridgnorth, and so on, and I have in mind a basic design for the new U. C. Sussex, a sketch of which could be sent in when invited. All my designs are simple and follow mediaeval coats in practicability.

So far as academical dress is concerned my normal invitation is to submit a memorandum on the subject, and then later to give a demonstration of possible systems. The academical dress com'tee or sub-com'tee, then chooses one that it likes, and a full set of models is made. Having done this for so many decades, the technique is well-established. It seems as if you must have got a Council now able to act.

Kind regards, Yours sincerely, Charles Franklyn

Once again, he was premature. Stone thanked him in a brief letter dated 23 February 1959, but pointed out that the Council had only just held its first meeting, and that matters other than academic dress would of necessity occupy it for the present. Franklyn then appears to have restrained himself for some months. The University College of Sussex came into legal existence on 20 May 1959, following the approval of the Charter and Statutes by the Privy Council. It had been anticipated that although an initial charter would allow it to become a University College, a second would be required to obtain University status.[8] In fact, a decision by the University Grants Committee quickly allowed such foundations to apply immediately for such a transformation, while the need for this second document was removed by the addition of proposals in the charter designed to safeguard academic standards.[9] By the summer, an application had been made by Sussex to the College of Arms (via Richmond Herald), for the grant of a coat of arms, but its draft was still under discussion.[10]

---

6   Formerly vice-chancellor of the University of Wales.

7   He must have meant Stone's letter of 28 April 1958; there is no record of correspondence dated 28 January 1959.

8   For a detailed resumé of these early years, see W. G. Stone, 'Steps Leading to the Foundation of the University', in Daiches, pp. 168–92.

9   The University of Sussex, SxUOS1/1/1/1–GB181. First Annual Report, 1959–60, p. 16. Without this ruling the new foundation would have been tied to the syllabuses of the University of London.

10 SxUOS1/1/1/1–GB181. First Annual Report, p. 17.

Joint scheme by Franklyn and Shaw

It is probable that Norman Hargreaves-Mawdsley[11] was already being considered as a designer for the University's academic dress, but no further relevant correspondence has been traced until February 1961, when George Shaw makes an unannounced entrance. Quite how he became involved has not been ascertained, but he had already submitted a proposed scheme based on a shade of claret, with sample hoods made up by Wippell & Co., all of which were rejected and appear to be lost.[12] Shaw therefore offered a modified system, featuring a colour he termed Sussex Blue, together with five sketches (Figs 1A–1E): 'I have used the pink shade for the Arts colour, as white (in a blue hood) would clash with several other University degrees … Wippells have made up, at my request, BA, MA, BSc and MSc hoods according to this scheme … I have also got an undergraduate gown in Sussex blue for you to see.'[13] Despite Shaw being the sole signatory, this is evidently a collaborative effort, and later correspondence (see below) makes a strong case for Franklyn as designer of these hoods, with bachelors allotted Burgon hoods [s2], masters the London shape [f3], and doctors the full Oxford hood [f5], all of which were Franklyn's favoured choices.[14]

Shaw's proposal

UNIVERSITY OF SUSSEX PROPOSED SCHEME OF ACADEMIC DRESS

GOWNS

Undergraduates

A gown of Sussex Blue rayon with short bell-shaped sleeves of the Oxford Scholars' type, with a 6" slit in the forearm seam.

Bachelors

A black gown of Russell cord with open sleeves of the Oxford BA shape, reaching to the hem of the gown. The forearm seam to be slit 6" from the outer edge, and with a black silk covered button at the top of the slit.

Masters

A black gown of Russell cord, Poplin or Ribbed Rayon. The sleeve to be of the Oxford MA shape i.e. closed, but with the end of the sleeve to be cut at a right angle on the outer edge and at an acute angle on the inner edge. The arm hole to be of the inverted-T type, with a black silk covered button at the top of the slit.

Doctors' Undress Gowns

A black gown of Poplin, Ribbed Rayon or Corded silk of the same shape as for masters, with the addition of a square flap collar over the yoke.

---

11 William Norman Hargreaves-Mawdsley (1921–80) was always known by his second name.

12 Kerr and Shaw, p. 10.

13 The University of Sussex, SxUOS1/1/1/17/24 (1961–66). Letter from Shaw to Fulton, 18 February 1961.

14 Shaw specifically acknowledges himself as designer of the gowns in his letter of 8 December 1961 (see below). Groves also notes that the proposed MA hood almost exactly replicates the MA of Malaysia, designed by Franklyn in 1949, and that both Shaw and Franklyn tended to prefer the Oxford shape for doctors' robes, though the chosen design parallels the London PhD. For a succinct assessment of this projected scheme, see Groves, pp. 74–75.

For PhD—a row of Doctors' lace (Cambridge style) round the edge of the collar and round the arm hole.

For other Doctors—the PhD gown with the addition of a row of lace down the facings of the gown.

PhD

A claret-coloured robe of the Cambridge Doctors' shape, with facings and sleeve linings of the University Colour silk (Sussex Blue), with a cord and button of the faculty colour at the elbow, and with a border 1" wide of the faculty colour down the inner margin of the facings.

Other Doctors

A scarlet cloth robe of the Cambridge doctors' shape, with facings and sleeve linings of the University colour silk, with a cord and button of the faculty colour at the elbow, and with a border 1" wide of the faculty colour down the inner margin of the facings.

HOODS
Bachelors.

A hood of Russell cord or ribbed rayon of the University colour, of the Oxford (Burgon) shape, lined with the faculty colour and edged with white fur. The neckband to be V-shaped and with a loop to hold it.

Masters

A hood of ribbed rayon of the University colour, of the Cambridge shape, with the corners of the cape rounded. The hood to be lined and edged ½" round the cape with the faculty colour.

The neckband as for bachelors.

Doctors

PhD—A claret cloth hood of the Oxford doctors' shape, lined with the University silk and with a border ½" wide inside and outside the hood proper of the faculty colour.

Other Doctors—A scarlet cloth hood of the Oxford doctors' shape lined with the University silk and with a border ½" wide inside and outside the hood proper of the faculty colour.

CAPS

Undergraduates, Bachelors and Masters—a black cloth Mortar board.
Doctors in Undress—a black velvet Mortar board.
Doctors in Full Dress—a round black velvet bonnet with cord and tassels of the faculty colour.

FACULTY COLOURS

Arts—Neyron Rose (B.C.C. 55)   Science—Deep Gold (B.C.C. 5)

This system would have resulted in a striking but not over-complicated set of robes, since the broad nature of the courses divided all the faculties into only two schools, thereby making them degree colours rather than faculty colours. Neyron Rose, a vivid

Figs 1A–1E. Shaw's sketches

Images reproduced by kind permission of University of Sussex Special Collections at The Keep

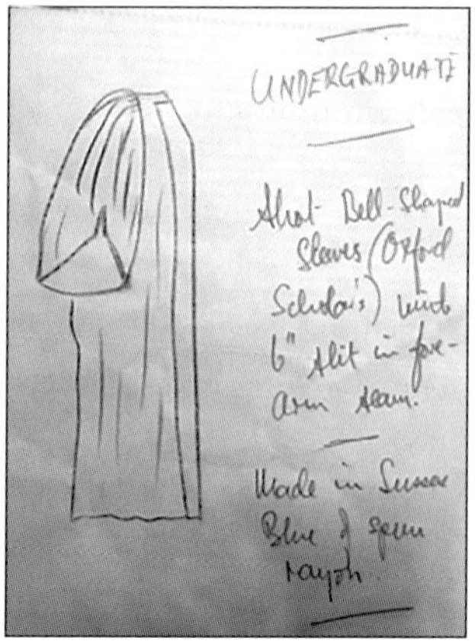

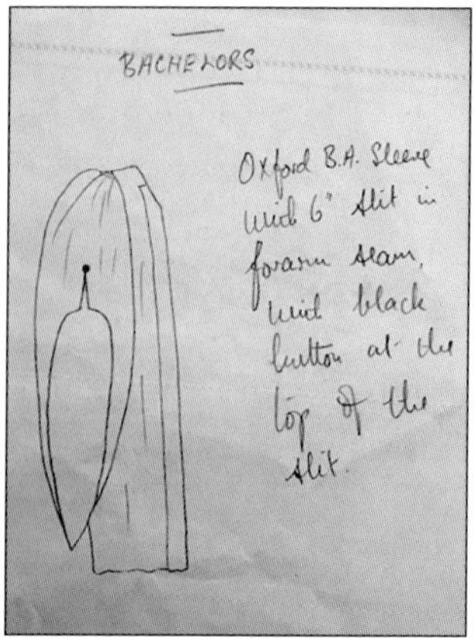

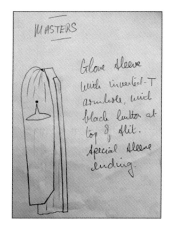

Fig. 1A. Undergraduates [u4], the Durham shape, in blue.

Fig. 1B. Bachelors [b7].

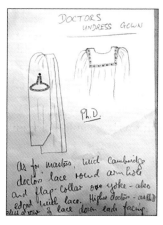

Fig. 1C. Masters [m16].

Fig. 1D. Doctors' undress gowns [d1].

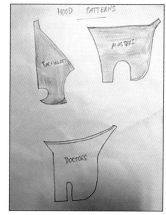

Fig. 1E. Shaw's sketch of hood patterns most probably designed by Franklyn.

pink or cerise (BCC 35, not 55) and Gold (BCC 6, not 5)[15] are very close to those allocated to the same faculties at Southampton, the dress of which—lest we forget—Franklyn was also responsible.[16]

The colour of Sussex Blue was not specified, but the prototype BSc hood has since come to light: a rich azure, edged with white fur (recalling sea-spray, perhaps?) (Fig. 2). This colour seems to have particularly appealed to Franklyn but his appropriation of it for the shell of the bachelors' and masters' hoods, as well as the inclusion of fur, are

15 For an assessment of the BCC colours and their adoption by universities worldwide, see Scott.

16 Neyron rose also features in the DSc robes for Cranfield, also an institution with only two faculties; was there some influence here?

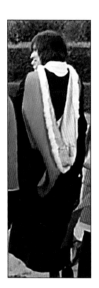

Fig. 2. The only known image of the prototype BSc hood (note the gold lining) for Sussex [s2], designed by Franklyn. The hood was gifted to John Balsdon but its current whereabouts are not known.

features that appear almost nowhere else in his designs.[17] They lend particular weight to the intimate connection he undoubtedly felt towards the university of his chosen county—as well, of course, to the intensity of his annoyance when his 'appeal to all lovers of what is beautiful and picturesque in academical dress'[18] was unequivocally rejected in favour of unorthodoxy.

The reply to Shaw has also not been traced. Did the authorities disapprove, were they urged to survey the field, or was there already a revolutionary streak in the upper hierarchy that was determined to depart from convention? In 1965, Shaw's Sussex gowns were offered to Bath and immediately incorporated into its initial scheme (1966), although they were dropped in 1997 in favour of more generic designs, perhaps for reasons of costs.[19]

Escalating persistence

Judicious discretion might have advanced Franklyn further, but was unrealistic to expect. He thanked Stone for his letter of 23 February, reiterated that he had designed for four British universities and written for three encyclopaedias, advised that his usual procedure was a demonstration of robes, and confided, 'I have one lovely silk up my sleeve for you. When do you expect your charter?'[20] The importance of this prized colour to Franklyn may be confirmed from his later oft-quoted lamentation: 'The present system is a calamity because the writer could have given Sussex the most beautiful robes of all, reminiscent of the blue-green of the sea and the green of the Downs.'[21] He referred to the sumptuous silk of peacock-blue shot green, designed in 1951 for The Australian National University, Canberra; its use there was prevented by import restrictions,[22] but he had already considered it for the University of Hull in 1954.[23] Franklyn was fond of stating that he had something up his sleeve, and would employ almost identical terms and catchphrases when negotiating an equally unsuccessful approach to the University of Warwick in 1963.[24] In the meantime, Stone must have decided that embryonic ceremonial was occupying far too much of his time, and the

17 Franklyn's only other known use of fur—and that probably imposed on him—was in 1949 for the bachelors' hoods of the renegade Western Orthodox University: Groves, p. 54. In 1995, Shaw noted (p. 3) that none of the new universities had used fur in their hoods, 'no doubt fearing the wrath of the so-called "animal rights" activists …'.

18 Franklyn, p. 12.

19 For further information and additional sketches of these gowns, see Ripley.

20 SxUOS1/1/1/17/24. Letter from Franklyn to Stone, 8 March 1961.

21 Franklyn, p. 208. See also Groves, pp. 67–68.

22 Haycraft, pp. 62, 160.

23 Baker, p. 35.

24 Jackson, 'Warwick', p. 20. This later saga closely mirrored Franklyn's tussles with Sussex and Essex, both in the phraseology of his own letters and the increasingly jaded responses of the exhausted recipients. See also Eggleston, p. 37.

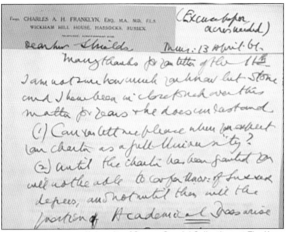

Fig. 3. Franklyn's letter of 13 April 1961, transcribed below.

matter was delegated to the registrar, Alfred Shields—who responded indifferently, implying ignorance of all previous exchanges. 'The College council has not yet given any attention to this particular subject, since such dress would not be required for over three years ... I shall see that your name is brought before the Council when the matter is eventually discussed.'[25]

This lethargic rejoinder provoked a frantic response, scribbled on the reverse of a commercial circular extolling the virtues of the drug Tenuate (Fig. 3).[26] A printed heading from Franklyn's own letterhead notepaper was pasted at the top of this makeshift stationery, an untidy idiosyncrasy in which he would still be indulging over three years later.[27] The unbounded devotion to his life's work was once again negated by his dogmatic approach, encapsulated by a wearisomely emphatic insistence (fiercely underlined on each occasion) on the adjective 'academical', not for the last time.

(Excuse paper, acres needed)

Thurs 13 April 1961
Dear Mr Shields,

[...] I am not sure how much you know but Stone and I have been in close touch over this matter for years & he does understand.

(1) Can you tell me please when you expect your charter as a full University?

(2) Until the charter has been granted you will not be able to confer Univ. of Sussex degrees, and not until then will the position of Academical Dress arise.

(3) I have designed the complete systems of Academical and Official Dress for 4 British Universities, and have a truly beautiful possibility up my sleeve for you if you do me the honour and give me the pleasure of laying a system before you.

Believe me, Yours sincerely, Charles Franklyn

Given Franklyn's proclivity in noting the exact time of arrival of his mail, his extreme rapidity in responding, and the all-too-regular and reliable postal service of the time, one may well imagine his correspondents dispatching what they fervently hoped were stalling replies, only to return home to find yet another self-aggrandizing epistle on the mat. There was simply no time for daily wrestling with such intractable and

25 SxUOS1/1/1/17/24. Letter from Shields to Franklyn, 11 April 1961.

26 Now a discredited treatment, but then available on prescription for women wishing to lose weight. The author is grateful to Dr Jane Mackay for clarification of this matter.

27 See report of his letter to the first vice-chancellor of the University of Warwick, in Groves, p. 5. Since Franklyn clearly had sufficient notepaper to prune and paste, it is impossible to fathom why he did not use it as intended, but his reasoning is now lost to posterity.

illegible obsessiveness, and Shields replied jadedly with an almost identical reiteration of his previous letter, advising that it was hoped the Charter would be granted before the first students arrived in October. Franklyn dispatched his next missive on receipt, pointing out the necessity of robes for inaugural ceremonies, of which fact the registrar was either unaware or chose to ignore.

Sat 15 April 1961
My dear Shields,

[…] May I tell you this (academical dress having been my special study and hobby since 1910, and being responsible for the articles on this subject in 'The Encyclopaedia Britannica' since 1941 June, & in 2 other encyclopaedias, as well as 'Grove's Dictionary of Music and Musicians', 5th edition)

I   Immediately a charter has been issued the Senate has appointed a sub-committee on Academical Dress. All the older universities have done this.

II   All Official Robes (Chancellor, Vice-Chancellor, Pro-Chancellor, Registrar, Treasurer, Librarian, Esquire Bedell etc) have to have robes designed at once, for the Inaugural Ceremonies. Academical Dress also has to be designed because at the inaugural ceremony some degrees are conferred 'honoris causa' (doctorates) & the Chancellor is always created DCL or LLD 'jure dignitatis' or 'hon. causa' at once.

III   I have a v. v. lovely colour up my sleeve for you and would give you a Demonstration of it. If you reject it another new university will have it.

With regards, Yours sincerely, Charles Franklyn

Shields did not wait for Franklyn to run out of sleeves, but escalated the correspondence to the principal, whose tentative enquiries [unsigned on copy] betrayed matters proceeding apace elsewhere. The priority was surely to reject Franklyn quickly without official culpability; but the inch allowed Franklyn to take the mile.

31 May 1961

I have seen the triangular correspondence between you, Stone and the Registrar. We are now beginning to turn our minds to the question of robes and academic dress generally. You will not be surprised to hear that we have had approaches from other quarters as well. In order that we may be in a position to discuss the problem with as full a knowledge as possible, I would be very grateful if you would, quite informally, tell me under what conditions you would be prepared to submit designs to us. For example, would you be interested in doing so only on the condition that we approached no one else; or would you be willing to submit them in competition with the designs of another?

The University of Sussex: Academical and Official Dress
My Dear Principal, […]

(1) It does not surprise to learn that approaches have been made from other quarters. My offer to help may have been the first as it was made as far back as 27 April 1958, and is very dear to my heart.

(2) It has never occurred to me to stipulate any conditions. I am entirely at your service and that of the Academical Dress or Sub-Committee of the Senate on Academical Dress, whatever it will be called. These Ac: Dress Committee are always perfectly free to see and to consider any proposals or suggestions laid before them.

(3) In designing the complete system of Academical Dress for 4 British Universities I have invariably been asked to give a full-dress Demonstration of the system suggested, and each Ac: Dress Committee has shown the very greatest interest

in these & has striven to obtain for each new University the most perfect and most distinct system—pride has been taken in this. In giving such Demonstrations a miscellaneous selection of other university robes and systems has been shown too so that comparisons may be made.

(4) My first requirements are

(a) a complete list of the degrees that the new University will be empowered to confer.

(b) any suggestions that you and your committee have in mind. These suggestions may be of vital importance e.g. Malaya told me at once that certain colours were barred in deference to Chinese customs. Black was completely barred, so were yellow, white, grey & crimson.

Hull decided to have all official robes in blue, not orthodox black.

Southampton decided to have all official robes in black damask as London.

Hull has begun BD, DD, BMus, DMus, (& theirs are the most beautiful in the world). Southampton has no degrees in Theology or Music. Neither grants any in Medicine. Malaya has degrees in Pharmacy & Engineering and these faculty colours I provided for them recently, adding to the 1949 system.

(c) To give an adequate Demonstration I need really for comfort 8 weeks notice.

(5) If the system I present were to be passed I would then draw up the complete Regulations for you to prevent abuses and degradation.

(6) Further, I would be very pleased at any time to study and consider with you any other suggestions made by anyone else, for (i) I might learn something or (ii) I might spot some defect or some infringement of some other institution.

(7) I do not fear competition. This has been my study since Sept: 1910 (51 years in Sept:) and I am confident that I can produce a system of which all would be continually proud. But in order to give you all that you wish to have it is essential that I should be advised if any wishes exist already that I should bear in mind.

[and 8 Yes, I follow Cambridge, our most accurate university where they insist upon Academical Dress like Ecclesiastical Dress! Please ask the typist to address envelopes as printed above!] [28]

With kind regards, Yours sincerely, Charles Franklyn.

'My first requirements are ...'—before anything had been decided or offered. If the principal steeled himself to read on, the forcefulness of the closing paragraphs must have decided what little there was left to decide. On 5 June, his secretary sent a brief acknowledgment, whereupon Franklyn urged that a demonstration might be managed in six weeks rather than eight, and broached the subject of the College Arms for a third time, closing with the preposterous assertion: 'The arms I designed for the University of Malaya is the best and simplest coat granted to any University since 1485.'[29] It is easy to imagine the vaunt doing the rounds of the Senior Common Room

---

28 SxUOS1/1/1/17/24. Letter from Franklyn to Fulton, 1 June 1961.

29 SxUOS1/1/1/17/24. Letter from Franklyn to the vice-chancellor's secretary, 6 June 1961. At some point during this extended broadside, Franklyn might have been expected to draw attention to his two heraldic dissertations in *The Illustrated London News*, but evidently chose not to do so. The first, on 24 November 1934, expounded on 'The Armorial Bearings of H.R.H. the Duke of Kent and H.R.H. Princess Marina of Greece and Denmark', and is startling for his observations concerning blue eyes and Nordic heritage, curiously reminiscent of the contemporary cultural obsessions of Percy Grainger: '... so that racially and heraldically the match is perfect'. More recently, on 14 May 1960, a two-page essay in the same magazine disparaged the arms of Princess Margaret and Antony Armstrong-Jones in familiar phrases.

before the principal turned frostier, pointing out that new Arms were being designed by his former pupil, Dr Anthony Wagner, already Richmond Herald and shortly to become Garter King of Arms. Wagner's impeccable credentials would have floored most, but distracted Franklyn not at all.

> My dear Principal, [...]
>
> (1) May I take it that my original reply was perfectly satisfactory? (June 1st)
>
> (2) Arms. I am sorry that you are already somewhat involved in this for 2 reasons.
>
> (a) I have a very fine simple design quite mediaeval in style for consideration.
>
> (b) If you apply for a Patent through Wagner, it will cost £100, and he is likely to ask £40 more for a certificate on vellum. If you ask for supporters too the cost might be £300. You would not know it but Arms COULD be [illegible] to the new University without cost. The E.M.[30] is able to GIVE you a warrant, as his father did for W. Sussex in 1889 and I have recently asked the E.M. about this and the idea attracted him. Until you have [illegible] Wagner's designs you are not committed.
>
> Yours sincerely, Charles Franklyn[31]

That afternoon Franklyn visited Shaw at Lancing College for a council of war, following which they took up cudgels jointly; but it is painfully apparent that open alliance with Franklyn now sealed Shaw's own fate as well. Both were swiftly informed that the overall position was quite clear and only awaited the committee's decision; but while Shaw then had the sense to hold his peace, Franklyn saw no reason to do anything of the kind.

> My Dear Principal, [...]
>
> (1) ARMS: if a proposed design has been duly signed and approved nothing more need be said. But it has been understood since time immemorial that until the Memorial (Petition) and the fees have been lodged, AND the proposed design approved and signed by the applicant, the Petitioner is committed to nothing. Wagner CAN design good arms but also he has designed some very bad ones (and even worse crests). Were you to see my design no harm would be done. Wagner cannot confer arms on anybody but can do no more than submit designs for consideration. And, if the University wishes to spend £200 it is fortunate that funds are available; but the E.M. COULD bestow arms upon the new university by Warrant as did his late father upon W. Sussex in 1889.
>
> Surely a great honour to derive arms from the E.M. himself? [I tried to be helpful]
>
> (2) Academical Dress: Yes, I have known George W. Shaw six years and have helped him as much as possible and he is acquiring a mastery of the subject. He telephoned me at 8.30 a.m. on Saturday, told me that he was very interested, knew, and had seen you, and he suggested that we should cooperate and endeavour to do the best possible. To this I assented very readily and with pleasure. He asked me over to Lancing and we spent some 4 hours on Saturday going over the ground & looking at models. He has some very good ideas.

---

30 Earl Marshal, being a hereditary title of the Dukes of Norfolk. As Head of the College of Arms, the fifteenth Duke, Henry Fitzalan-Howard, did indeed pay for most of the cost of having the County Council's arms approved in 1889 (one of the first following the Local Government Act that year). These were superseded in 1974, but all had, in fact, been used and attributed long before official recognition. It must be presumed that Franklyn had discussed the matter with the sixteenth Duke when visiting the College.

31 SxUOS1/1/1/17/24. Letter from Franklyn to Fulton, 10 June 1961.

We would like, therefore, to give you and your Committee a joint Demonstration. This would be comprehensive and should give your Committee the greatest help. It would also effect economies in several ways. I understand that you are not keen on the standard black hoods for bachelors and masters, and it is true that something much more beautiful can be devised.

With kind regards, Yours sincerely, Charles Franklyn[32]

A comparable browbeating lecture was posted to the chancellor-elect, Viscount Monckton, who consulted with Fulton as how best to reply: 'We shall no doubt hear from him again. These troubles we must bear with patience.'[33] On 11 August he reiterated to Franklyn that the Committee was considering the matter, which merely gifted his opponent two targets rather than one. The following day, Franklyn reminded Monckton that he was awaiting an invitation for a demonstration of robes—none such had been promised[34]—and recalled his proposed cooperation with Shaw: 'Together we could help greatly.' The haranguing of Fulton then resumed.

My dear Vice-Chancellor,
Academical Dress
[...] Referring to your kind letter of June 12th now that you have had your charter some 5 weeks, I am hoping that you have set up, or will do so shortly, your sub-committee of the Senate (or Council) on academical dress. From 50 years study of the subject, I believe that a committee would have the best chance of adopting the finest proposals if a full-scale Demonstration were given, so that they could study various suggestions in the flesh, actually seeing them in real life, and not mere paper suggestions. Usually I show some £500 worth of robes, existing systems and suggested systems.

It would help greatly if you have any ideas ('pro' or 'contra') if you would be so good as to tell me what they are, e.g. if you are dead against any shot silk being used or, if you are opposed to bachelors & masters having standard orthodox hoods, black outside. If you prefer coloured hoods this would help—as I mentioned, there is one most lovely silk available, adopted by a university in a great Dominion, then stopped because of ex pat restrictions, & a horrible heavy blue wool cloth was adopted instead.[35] If you are not opposed to a lovely shot silk this (unique) is available still, but York, Norwich, or one of the others might seize it if they got the chance.[36]

George Shaw and I are anxious to collaborate.

With kind regards, Yours sincerely, Charles Franklyn[37]

Initial decisions

The Royal Charter creating the University of Sussex was received in August 1961, and the institution opened in October of that year, occupying temporary premises in Pres-

---

32 SxUOS1/1/1/17/24. Letter from Franklyn to Fulton, 13 June 1961.

33 SxUOS1/1/1/17/24. Letter from Monckton to Fulton, 10 August 1961. Monckton had previously been president of the University College.

34 As shown in his correspondence with Oxford twenty years earlier, it was entirely characteristic of Franklyn to suggest a certain course, and then immediately act as if this had already been adopted.

35 Confirmation of Franklyn's intention to give Sussex the shot silk originally designed for ANU.

36 They did not, of course, get the chance, because Franklyn did not design for them, or for any further foundations.

37 SxUOS1/1/1/17/24. Letter from Franklyn to Fulton, 17 September 1961.

ton Road, Brighton, until the main campus was complete.[38] Matters elsewhere were already advanced, as the Annual Report noted.

> Designs for the remaining items of academic dress (bachelors' and masters' gowns and hoods) were finally approved during the year by the Senate Committee appointed for that purpose, in consultation with Dr W. N. Hargreaves-Mawdsley. Considerable discussion went on during the year between representatives of the Union and representatives of the Senate as to the occasions when academic dress should be worn. It was generally agreed that students would not be expected to wear their gowns on any but formal academic occasions, and it was left to the Senate, in consultation with the Union, to prescribe what occasions should be regarded academic for this purpose.[39]

The reference to 'remaining items' indicates that designs of robes for officials, doctors and undergraduates had been agreed, although not produced: a report of the first meeting of the Court of Sussex University noted that Lord Monckton, the new chancellor, was 'as yet unrobed'.[40] On 22 November, the news of Hargreaves-Mawdsley's appointment was broken to Franklyn, whose scorching rejoinder emphasized his inevitable and intractable refusal to admit defeat.

> Dear Vice-Chancellor,
> Academical Dress
>   Your letter of yesterday has given me a shock. I have had the University of Sussex very much in mind for 3½ years, and now it seems I am turned down flat and barred out![41]
>   I know the name Hargreaves Mawsdly but what he has to do with academical dress I do not know: I do not know of him as an established authority on the subject.[42] Do you know whether he is responsible for articles on the subject in

---

38 Gray, p. 9. The early years of the foundation, including details of its unconventional course structures, comprising a central core subject with additional papers setting the main study in context, are documented in Daiches. The innovative curriculum drew on such Oxford courses as PPE and was delivered very much on traditional Oxbridge lines, with voluntary attendance at lectures and a tutorial system requiring weekly essays for discussion. The system gradually fell by the wayside as funding declined, although it was partly the reason for the tag 'Balliol by the Sea' coined on the very day that the Royal Charter was incorporated (*The Times*, 16 August 1961). It would also be termed 'The Pink Brick University' and as well as 'the best thing that has happened to Brighton since the wicked Prince Regent chose the town for his orgies' (*Sunday Times*, 14 July 1963).

39 SxUOS1/1/1–GB181. Second Annual Report, 1961, p. 39. At the Second Meeting of Senate on 10 October 1961, it had also been agreed that faculty members should wear gowns when lecturing during the session 1961–62, although this requirement was rescinded at the Ninth Meeting, 19 June 1962.

40 *The Times*, 11 November 1961.

41 A paragraph that would resurface just over two years later in Franklyn's lament to the vice-chancellor of Essex on being rejected as designer for that university also; see Groves, p. 78.

42 This is entirely implausible. It seems the two men did not meet until 1962, but Hargreaves-Mawdsley began his postgraduate research in 1955, and was awarded his DPhil on academic and legal dress in 1958. The thesis was embargoed in perpetuity at Hargreaves-Mawdsley's own request, so still cannot be consulted, but most of it appeared in the two volumes subsequently published by Clarendon Press, in which Franklyn is cited as one having given exceptional assistance. This endeavour apparently ended Franklyn's own doctoral aspirations at a stroke, and his lofty condescension not only betrayed his fragility but undermined his credibility,

any Encyclopaedia or other ref. works?[43] I believe that if he is a genial, kindly and broad-minded man anxious to get the best result, he would welcome collaboration with me (and with Dr George W. Shaw too, also turned down I suppose.)

We have been at work on your problem a long time and many models have been made up. I have asked you to be so good as to let me know when your Sub-Committee on Academical Dress has been appointed and then, IF I may give them a full-scale Demonstration, showing existing systems, possible systems, and a suggested system.[44] It can hardly be beneficial to a new university and her future graduates if two experts are barred out and are not even allowed to show or suggest anything. I know of no reason why you should not coopt Shaw and me to your sub-committee, for we are highly qualified university graduates and are experts. We would, too, have a chance to see & criticize H-M's suggested plan on paper.

Kind regards, Yours sincerely, Charles Franklyn[45]

The above letter is addressed to the vice-chancellor; but, in another example of triangular correspondence, it must have been forwarded to Viscount Monckton—who, in a letter from his private secretary to Fulton, sought advice before replying. In a subsequent tactful apology to Franklyn, he pointed out that as the decision had been made by the proper bodies, he was unable, as chancellor, to interfere in matters appropriate to committees. His salutation to 'Mr Franklyn' evidently elicited a typically irascible rebuke,[46] since Monckton passed it to Fulton on 12 December, remarking helplessly, 'I will excuse myself about the nomenclature, but I thought from the printed heading that he preferred to be called Esq. As for the rest, what would you have me say?'

I am sorry that you have been further troubled by Franklyn. He has been on the telephone at length with me and with Stone. His letter, I fear, bears out all the warnings that we received in advance. What is abundantly clear—and I have checked the records very closely—is that at no time has he been given any encouragement to suppose that he would be asked to design our academic dress. Others beside Dr Franklyn wrote and offered their services. The decision has gone in favour of a younger man, Hargreaves-Mawdsley, who is writing the history of academic dress for the Oxford University Press and to whom we propose to pay a fee of 100 guineas (just as we are paying a fee to the Garter King of Arms for designing our coat of arms). My feeling is that it is no use taking up his points one by one and answering them in a letter. He is prepared to spend all his time in this argument and we should be absorbed to a quite unjustifiable extent in an unprofitable correspondence. So my feeling is that you should reply that you are very sorry there is nothing you could add to what you said in your previous letter. I am so sorry that you are being troubled in this way.[47]

since it is surely impossible to imagine him encountering Hargreaves-Mawdsley in any other field. Both he and Shaw often misspelled the name.

43 A typically double-edged enquiry, since Franklyn himself had composed the relevant entry for *Encyclopaedia Britannica* since 1941, and was about to assume responsibility for *Chambers*'s as well.

44 Two more typical turns of phrase: a breezy reference to a hypothetical committee before its establishment was even agreed or reported, let alone imminent; and the implication that he and Shaw had been working on the scheme in some official capacity, when (as far as is known) even Shaw had not been so engaged.

45 SxUOS1/1/1/17/24. Letter from Franklyn to Monckton, 23 November 1961.

46 This has not survived.

47 SxUOS1/1/1/17/24. Letter from Fulton to Monckton, 22 December 1961.

A very possible source of the warnings is the then vice-chancellor of the University of Southampton, David James. In 1964, he would advise John Butterworth (first vice-chancellor of the University of Warwick) to exercise strong caution when dealing with Franklyn, and it seems that the latter's greatly self-lauded scheme for Southampton, featuring swathes of appropriately named peacock-blue, was dearly bought in terms of relationships.[48] For an inexperienced committee pressed for time, the choice of a designer must have been a foregone conclusion. Hargreaves-Mawdsley was simply the least troublesome, his pedigree (after Oxford, he had just begun a research fellowship at the University of Edinburgh) and publication contract almost irrelevant. George Shaw was also bitter: 'I felt sure that … you were at least in favour of the black gowns which I designed'[49]—a remark that strengthens earlier speculation that the hoods were Franklyn's proposals. Shaw also asked to see Hargreaves-Mawdsley's scheme, but it is apparent that he did not receive a reply. The details were circulated at the fifth Meeting of Senate (23 January 1962).

Hargreaves-Mawdsley's initial scheme

ACADEMICAL DRESS FOR THE UNIVERSITY OF SUSSEX

Undergraduates
No headdress.
A black cloth gown without sleeves, simply holes for the passage of the arms. Knee-length. Cut away at the collar with a broad square piece of stuff (edged with the faculty colour (Arts: ultramarine (PhD.: navy blue), Science: gamboge, Laws: buff, Music: grey, Medicine: lavender, Divinity: violet) let in between the shoulders, the gown being gathered into small folds round this square. Open in front without facings.

Bachelors of Arts
Headdress, a square cap (mortar board) with a button, and with a border of black alpaca round the bottom edge of the head-piece.
A black cloth gown with a cut away collar and a yoke rounded at the bottom, the gown being pleated round this yoke. The sleeves to be bell-sleeves of moderate length with very sharply pointed ends, with a wide but not long vertical opening halfway down their length for the passage of the arms. Decorated on each sleeve above the arm-holes with a piece of twisted silk cord looped in the shape of the decoration on a bandsman's sleeve—this last indicating the BA.[50]
Hood, black cloth lined and edged with light grey fur in squares. Medium length with narrow square-ended liripipe.

Bachelors of Science
The same except the sleeves are to be decorated with a horizontal piece of black silk with three black buttons spaced out on the line of black silk; and the hood to be lined and edged with tawny fur in squares.

---

48 Jackson, 'Warwick', p. 15. This was not new: a warning about Franklyn's proclivity for tireless and persistent correspondence had been dispatched in 1953 from the registrar of Southampton to the registrar of University College, Hull: see Baker, pp. 32–33; also, Groves, pp. 16–17.

49 SxUOS1/1/1/17/24. Letter from Shaw to Fulton, 8 December 1961.

50 Hargreaves-Mawdsley meant the faculties, not the level of degree, since the MA and MSc gowns have the same decorations as those for the equivalent bachelors. Note that the distinctive pointed ends of the Sussex bachelors' robes were present from the earliest stages of the design.

Masters of Arts

A black cloth gown with cut-away collar and yoke in the form of a double bracket e.g. ⌣⌣ gathered below and at the shoulders. Black silk facings in front. The gown to be ankle-length (or thereabouts). Sleeves to be as long as the gown, panelled in type (i.e. square and sewn up below the arms), with broad square flat ends, with a broad but not long vertical opening half-way down for the passage of the arms. Decoration on the sleeve the same as BA.

Hood, black alpaca lined (but not edged) with ultramarine white striped (vertically) ribbed silk. Headdress, a black square cap with button and tassel.

Masters of Science

As above. Decoration on the sleeves as Bachelor of Science.

Hood, black alpaca, lined with gamboge ribbed silk.

Doctors of Philosophy

For special occasions: hard black domed biretta with ultramarine button on top. The biretta to be made of silk mohair gummed on to paste-board. For ordinary occasions the ordinary black mortar board with button and tassel, the button being navy blue, but the tassel black.

For ordinary occasions a black silk gown like that of MA., except that (1) the bottom edges of the sleeves are to be serrated, and (2) instead of the sleeve decoration of MA. is to be substituted one horizontal line of navy blue silk with three navy blue buttons and with a small navy blue tassel hanging from each of the three navy blue buttons.

For important occasions, together with the biretta, a silk robe of exactly the same shape as the undress gown, but the whole to be navy blue in colour, and instead of a cut-away collar to have a collar high and upstanding at the back and coming down to join the facings in front. On the right shoulder a thin band of scarlet silk fastened on the top of the shoulder by means of a scarlet button, the ends hanging down back and front. No decorations on sleeves and no hood.

Doctors of Laws

As above, but the button on the biretta and on the square cap to be buff. The undress gown to be decorated on the sleeves with a horizontal line of buff silk with buff buttons and tassels. The full dress gown as of the Doctor of Philosophy shape, but of buff silk.

Doctors of Science

The same except that the button on the biretta and on the square cap, the decorations on the sleeves, and the colour of the full dress robe to be gamboge.

Doctors of Letters

The same except that the button on the biretta and on the square cap, the decorations on the sleeves of the undress gown, and the colour of the full dress robe to be dark green with blue lights.

The Vice-Chancellor

On ordinary occasions, whatever degree he happens to have. On very formal occasions, a robe in shape exactly like the full dress robe of Doctors, but without the button and scarlet band on the shoulder. The robe to be plum-coloured silk with a scarlet cape over shoulders. Black biretta with black button.

The Chancellor

A black silk gown like that of the Doctors' undress gown decorated round the lower edge of the yoke, on the sleeves above the arm-holes (where the decorations is [*sic*] to consist of three horizontal strips of silk each with three buttons and three tassels), below the arm-holes, and at the bottom of the sleeves, and the facings, with gold braid. On the right shoulder of his robe a gold and enamel brooch of the University arms. His biretta is to be like that of a doctor, but it is to have a thick band of gold braid surrounding its base, and its button is to be gold.

REMARKS

May I suggest that it is to be insisted on that the dress of the highest degree which the wearer possesses is always worn?

May I also suggest that when someone from outside enters a post in the University of Sussex he should begin to wear the dress of the degree of the University of Sussex equivalent to that which he holds at another university? The bad habit is growing up in the provincial universities of wearing at their ceremonies the dress of their original university, so spoiling the uniformity.

In my opinion it would be a good idea if the University of Sussex became as exclusive in this way as Oxford and Cambridge.

I suggest that with full dress a long white tie with a white collar should be worn. This to me seems the best modern compromise. Ordinary ties of various colours are ugly and clash with robes.

W. N. H-M.

The inventiveness of this vivid proposal raises as many questions as it answers. The school colours anticipated some faculties not then established, such as Music and Medicine, but other choices are eccentric: buff for Law, ultramarine stripes for the MA, plum and scarlet for the vice-chancellor, and a green doctors' robe with its 'blue lights'.[51] The reasoning behind such flamboyancy will be considered, although it says much for the resilience of Senate that general approval was granted.[52] Eight university representatives, few with any especial expertise in the subject, then convened as a sub-committee to debate everything further. Hargreaves-Mawdsley, in attendance as the nominal consultant, must have felt as if he were undergoing a viva, particularly as he was not acknowledged as the designer, but merely as one who 'had been invited to suggest designs'. A later meeting, in 1964, decreed that both BA and BSc hoods should be the same; so although it is remarkable to learn of the proposed BSc with squares of tawny fur, the item was probably never made.

Sub-Committee re Academic Dress
Minutes of a meeting held at the Old Ship Hotel at 7:30 p.m. on 6th February 1962

1. The Vice-Chancellor (Chairman), Professor Asa Briggs, Professor J. P. Corbett, Professor D. Daiches, Dr A.M. Ross, Dr A K Thorlby, Professor M Wight and the Registrar. Dr W. N. Hargreaves-Mawdsley, who had been invited to suggest designs for the academic dress of the University, also attended the meeting.

2. Dr Hargreaves-Mawdsley explained his proposed designs, and said that he had attempted to get away from the conventional 19th century pattern adopted by most other British Universities, and had suggested designs based on mediaeval European practice. During the discussion, the following points were made: —

---

51 It is curious that the colours for Letters were different to those of the Arts faculty, but unclear whether they comprised a variety of shot silk, or some additional decoration.

52 SxUOS1/1/2/27/3/1-14. Fifth Meeting of Senate, 23 January 1962.

(1) Caps
   (a) It is essential to ensure that all caps, especially the birettas, can be raised from the head without difficulty.
   (b) It was suggested that women undergraduates should have soft hats rather than mortar-boards; it was agreed that the views of women members of Council, staff (if any), and students should be obtained on this point.
   (c) It was agreed that undergraduates should not have any form of head-dress.
   (d) The tassels of the caps worn by bachelors and masters should be coloured to represent their Schools of Study.

(2) Gowns
   The edging of undergraduate gowns should be braided from the School colour, together with the Faculty colour. It was suggested that the undergraduates' views might be obtained on these gowns.

(3) Hoods
   The hoods for bachelors and masters should be edged with the School colour.

(4) Colours
   Some doubt was expressed about the suitability of buff as the Law Faculty colour, the LL.D. gown being the one most likely to be seen at honorary degree ceremonies. It was suggested that a stronger colour be selected for Law; e.g. the Law colour might be gamboge and the Science colour tawny (instead of buff and gamboge respectively).

(5) Vice-Chancellor's Dress
   It was noted that the Vice-Chancellor had already had a gown made up, and therefore the dress proposed by Dr Hargreaves-Mawdsley could not be adopted. It was, however, suggested that the existing gown might be used for functions outside the University, and another type of dress might be prescribed for internal functions; however, the Vice-Chancellor stated that in that case he would probably want Dr Hargreaves-Mawdsley to modify his proposals for the 'internal' dress.

(6) Chancellor's Dress
   It was agreed that the Chancellor himself should be consulted about Dr Hargreaves-Mawdsley's proposals.
   Dr Hargreaves-Mawdsley agreed to consider all the above points and modify his proposals, where necessary, in accordance therewith.

4. It was agreed that Dr Hargreaves-Mawdsley should arrange with Messrs. Ede & Ravenscroft to make up one hood and gown of each type, and to obtain samples of the colours proposed for the others. The sub-committee would then inspect these before further action was taken.
In the meantime, the registrar should explain what had been done to the local firms which had indicated an interest in this matter and discuss with them the possibility of stocking undergraduate gowns only.
5. In the course of the discussions, the following points arose also: -

   (1) The sub-committee was not in favour of Dr Hargreaves-Mawdsley's suggestion that members of the faculty of the University of Sussex should

wear the University's own academic dress, and not the dress of the University at which they graduated, and Dr Hargreaves-Mawdsley withdrew this suggestion.

(2) It was agreed to recommend that on formal occasions, a white collar and white bow-tie should be worn with academic dress.

(3) It was suggested that undergraduates be not allowed to wear a gown until they have passed the preliminary Examination, and that gowns be formally presented by the University at the end of the second term to those passing the examination.

Battering rams

In the midst of these fraught analyses, the indefatigable Franklyn elected to redouble (for at least the fifteenth time) his vigorous assaults on topics that had long been resolved, while simultaneously berating the principal's distinguished former pupil.

Wednesday 14 February 1962
My dear Vice-Chancellor,

(1) ARMS: I understand that although the Letters Patent have not been issued yet that the final design of the arms is just about settled.[53] May I see the proposed design please, before the design has been embodied and blazoned in the Patent. I trust that a shield of Arms only will be granted, which is the correct practice for a university, college, school, diocese etc? Anthony Wagner has designed some 'shockers' (e.g. look in 'Debrett' at the hopeless & characterless arms granted to Lord Attlee). Recently I have designed arms for Lord [illegible], the Queen's gynaecologist, the Prime Minister & physician Lord Brain and others. [T.S., Canford School, St Peter's Hall, Oxford, Borough of Bridgnorth, R. Dental Hosp. etc etc.] All fees are going up on April 1st.

(2) Academical Dress. Mr W. Hargreaves-Mawdesley has been appointed, commissioned, employed (=paid) to draw up and submit a suggested system of Academical & Official dress, presumably this has been typed or even printed for your sub-committee to consider, adopt, adopt in part, modify or reject, may I please see the proposed system?

I shall be over in Hove one day before February is out, so could I fit this in with a call on you and do two calls on the same journey? The difficulty of providing a beautiful system that does not infringe existing robes is great: shapes too need to be considered, and I hope that you have not considered any doctors' full dress robes of the wrong shape (sleeves) forbidden [at] the Hampton Court conference of 1603?[54]

Yours sincerely, Charles Franklyn

Fulton's secretary responded on 16 February, regretting that the vice-chancellor was unable to meet as he was in London for the next few weeks. At this entirely reasonable excuse, Franklyn—doubtless envisaging the long-pursued quarry slipping through his fingers—unleashed a splenetic scrawl at the very borders of legibility, recalling Clive James's immortal phrase, 'Even in moments of tranquillity, [he] sounds like a man whose trousers are on fire.'

---

53 The arms of the University of Sussex can be seen at <www.sussex.ac.uk/broadcast/read/60928> [retrieved 17 December 2023].

54 In fact, 1604, since the schedule for the previous November was postponed by an outbreak of bubonic plague.

Saturday 17 February 1962
Dear Miss Whitbourne,

[...] I expect that your V-C will be returning to Hove to sleep each night. I am anxious to make a definite appointment to see him as soon as possible, when convenient. To make it easy to arrange, may I suggest that you phone me any morning between 10:00 to 10:30 a.m. when I can answer the ring at once. I have not yet found an elusive V-C nor any V-C who refused to see me & in fact I have lunched, dined & had tea with V-Cs and have found them all charming and accessible. As a member of four universities & a graduate of three of them (one 'hon. causa') I would expect pleasure & interests in a meeting.[55] Please do not wait until we are told that he has gone abroad for the month's vacation. And in the meantime, please tell me about the suggested design of the arms & the suggested academical dress [four illegible words][56]

Yours sincerely, Charles Franklyn

A pencilled note on the card states: 'Rang and said it would not be possible to arrange an appointment within the next few weeks. 23/2/62.'

Sunday 1 April 1962
Dear Miss Whitbourne,

May I remind you of your letter of Feb. 16th? I am waiting still for you to be so good as to tell me when the V-C would be pleased to see me. I am at his disposal at any time (except Monday 9th when I am entertaining real Sussex Saxons from Edinburgh. I will have to be most informal, so that if the V-C cared to ask me over to Hove, so near for me, to lunch or even tea on a Saturday, I would be available. I am quite used to having lunch, tea & dinner with V-Cs, Pro-Cs etc. There is sure to be plenty of time in April and I have heard from two other men holding important educational posts that he does wish to see me. [...]

Yours sincerely, Charles Franklyn

Two weeks elapsed before space was found in the vice-chancellor's diary to propose an appointment for 19 April. After all the effortful months, this would have been Franklyn's first meeting with Fulton, but it was insufficient. His own timetable was paramount.

Friday 13 April 1962
Dear Miss Whitbourne [...]

Now pray do not think that I am awkward. I am not, but am very freely available. To get over to you by 11:30 a.m. would mean my laying aside the whole of my work for a day, for the morning is as precious as food. From lunchtime onwards I can be free almost at any time, up to 11.p.m.

To get to you by 11:30 a.m. would mean the expense of a taxi, 9/6d at least, and then I could get myself back somehow. If I am to have a normal lunch here at 1:15, the ideal time to get over to you would be 3.0—4.0 p.m. if you would be so good as to tell me how to get to & to find Stanmer House. Do please try to find me an afternoon appt.

Yours sincerely, Charles Franklyn
Tea with the V-C would be the ideal arrangement.

_____

55 Franklyn was a member of Exeter College, Oxford (1940), a graduate of London and Lausanne, and holder of a degree *honoris causa* from Malaya.

56 Wagner's design had long been finalized and would be officially granted on 15 March, but once again Franklyn dismissed everything as 'suggested', persuading himself that matters which only he could resolve were still at an elementary stage.

On 17 April, the secretary advised that it would not be possible to arrange an afternoon appointment 'for a little time, but I will try to arrange something as soon as possible. Please do not trouble to reply to this letter; I will write again when an opportunity occurs.'

In the meantime, Arthur Knott, director of Wippell & Co., had contacted Fulton on 14 April, offering to quote against Hargreaves-Mawdsley's scheme, no doubt with a view to his firm being appointed official robemakers. The unsigned reply (19 April) remarked that the scheme was being considered, and the preparation of prototype robes with another firm[57] was already being arranged. An update soon appeared.

> The Council commissioned Dr W. N. Hargreaves-Mawdsley, of Oxford, an authority on academic dress, to design a series of gowns, hoods, etc. for the University. A design for an undergraduate gown, proposed by Dr Hargreaves-Mawdsley, was accepted and the Senate decided that this gown should be worn on official occasions, such as graduation ceremonies, examinations, leave-takings, University Church services, and such other occasions as might be prescribed.[58]

Shaw viewed the samples—presumably at Ede & Ravenscroft in Cambridge—and ensured that Fulton had no doubt as to the extent of his indignation.

> Dear Mr Fulton,
>
> I have now seen the academical robes designed for you by Hargreaves-Mawdesly, and feel that I must make some comment on them.
>
> The undergraduate gown is much too simple and completely lacking in dignity. Students will, of course, make their own gowns rather than pay 50/- or so for such a garment, with the result that all sorts of variations will be introduced.[59]
>
> Why is the bachelors' gown not correctly pleated at the back? You have adopted a new and specific type of yoke for masters and doctors, why not have the same for bachelors?
>
> Doctors robes—should have the correct shape of sleeve for a doctor as laid down at the Hampton Court Conference in 1604, and not the masters' sleeve.[60] And why have the small red ribbon on the shoulder? If you want to follow the French system, then why not give doctors a decent sized époge [*sic*] showing the faculty colour, and which could be worn with the undress gown? I cannot help feeling that your graduates, if and when they proceed to a doctorate will be rather angry to find

---

57 Ede & Ravenscroft.

58 SxUOS1/1/1/1–GB181. Third Annual Report, 1961–62, p. 20. This had been passed at the Sixth Meeting of Senate (20 February 1962), with a reinforced directive at the Seventh Meeting (27 March 1962): 'No candidate will be admitted to the examination room unless he is wearing a gown.' At the Ninth Meeting (19 June 1962) it was further agreed that present undergraduates must obtain their gowns before 16 October, and that future students should do so at the commencement of their first term.

59 The skimpy design [u6] certainly cannot hold a candle to Shaw's original proposal and its later unpopularity is unsurprising. Lacking even such enlivening features as the streamers of an Oxford commoner's gown, it is more reminiscent of a nineteenth-century Cambridge sizar's garb, sleeveless and without the pensioners' velvet on the facings. See in Jackson, *Ackermann, Cambridge*, Plate XIV.

60 Shaw and Franklyn had evidently discussed this point, but the present author has not sourced it. The Conference touched on surplices, square caps and 'men in turky gowns' (i.e., four Puritans), but no prescriptive directions concerning sleeves have yet come to light. See Humbert.

no dignified scarlet cloth robe, but only a yellow or green silk pantomime outfit. I am relieved to hear that you have decided to eliminate the four jesters' points from the bottom of the masters and doctors' sleeves, and to abolish the bowler hat for doctors.

The most ludicrous part of the whole scheme of course is the 'system' (if one can call it such) of hoods. These grey squares of nylon fur and the ladies' dress material of navy blue with white stripes might be costumes from the Micado! What is the connection between BA (grey fur), MA (navy blue with white stripes) and DLitt (dark green)? The whole thing is a jumble of disconnected bits and pieces. Your committee should have had several alternative schemes to see instead of being foisted off with this stuff. Already people in Cambridge—where these things are actually made—are laughing about it all. But I for one do not find it amusing, and can only hope that the other new universities will not make the same dreadful mistakes.

Yours sincerely, Geo. W. Shaw[61]

In the most regrettable absence of any written elucidations from the designer himself, what indeed is the connection? What reasoning may be deduced, what scheme estimated, to explain the apparent hodgepodge?

Heraldry and stained glass

During the revival of interest in medieval Oxford in the second half of the eighteenth century, Merton College attracted particular attention for its antiquity and fabric.[62] In his standard work on academic dress, at the very beginning of his chapter on Great Britain and Ireland, Hargreaves-Mawdsley draws attention to the twenty-four stained-glass windows (twenty-one now survive) in the College chapel, commemorating the donor Henry Mansfield,[63] each showing a scholar dressed in a 'wide-sleeved supertunica' and an almuce or amess, a garment usually made of squares of grey squirrel fur or marten's fur.[64] These thirteenth-century depictions of academic dress are some of the oldest to be found anywhere; but, to begin with dissent, his descriptions do not, in fact, bear detailed inspection, and recent scholarship has taken issue with them. Each image shows a *cappa clausa* with a hood, sometimes lined with fur, but nothing resembling an almuce as now understood.[65] Equally slender is Hargreaves-Mawdsley's contention that these images depict robes of the chancellor, a theory which arose long before the date of the glass could be established with certainty, or even confirmation that the chancellor had any distinguishing attire at the time.[66] A much closer representation of such is a manuscript initial from the Chancellor's Book in the Archives of Oxford University (1375), showing the chancellor, William de Wilton, receiving a charter from Edward III, wearing what is clear-

---

61 SxUOS1/1/1/17/24. Letter from Shaw to Fulton, 14 August 1962.

62 Ayers, Part 1, p. cxxx.

63 The windows are older than he states. Each bears the declaration *Magister Henricus de Mamesfeld me fecit*.

64 Hargreaves-Mawdsley, p. 60.

65 Ayers, p. 53—although Ayers was unaware that some points in his reappraisal of the Merton glass had already been addressed: see Kerr, p. 112. For a recent depiction of almuces, see the photograph of them worn by the Chapter of SS. John Baptist & John Evangelist, Regensburg, Bavaria (*c.* 2000) at <www.newliturgicalmovement.org> [retrieved 13 July 2023].

66 Ayers, p. lxxxix.

ly an almuce[67]—which Hargreaves-Mawdsley there attributes to his 'ecclesiastical standing.'[68] This odd confusion does not seem to have perplexed Hargreaves-Mawdsley at all when citing very similar examples elsewhere (he even includes a perfectly clear illustration of the *cappa clausa*),[69] but does not diminish his work in identifying distinctions between different degrees or scholastic hierarchy.

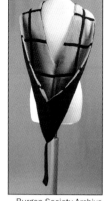

Fig. 4. Sussex's bachelors' hood.

Whatever the cause of this uncertainty, it seems highly likely—as Bruce Christianson has percipiently speculated[70]—that the almuce in this form was the origin of the grey nylon squares appearing on the hoods of Sussex bachelors; moreover, the intention to evoke miniver of some description is given additional credence by Hargreaves-Mawdsley's proposed use of tawny fur as well as grey. The use of fur on academic dress generally may also be put into context:

> ... the rule both at Oxford and Cambridge was that a bachelor's hood must be lined with the fur of some animal indigenous to the British Isles unless he was a nobleman, when the lining might be of silk.[71]

This ordinance is sourced by Franklyn to a statute of Henry VIII;[72] which (as Noel Cox suggests) is an indication that, by the sixteenth century, furs were most probably prominent features of graduate hoods, 'a sign of degree status ... those of graduates were furred or lined with fur or other material, such as stuff.'[73] In referring to the quires of collegiate and cathedral churches, Franklyn also quotes: '...in the fourteenth and following centuries, canons of the upper grade used the grey amess, made of grey squirrel outside and lined with miniver.'[74]

Different furs were therefore signifiers of social status. Atchley's remarks on the dress of Cardinal College, Oxford (now Christ Church), must also be noted, even though he refers to ecclesiastical dress, since it is already quite evident that historical fidelity mattered less to Hargreaves-Mawdsley than appearance:

> The dean and superior canons wore surplices and grey amesses; the minor canons surplices and hoods of blue-coloured cloth *fashioned in semblance of amesses* [italics mine] and fringed along the lower border with sky blue or grey fur.[75]

It is a firm supposition of this article that Hargreaves-Mawdsley's scheme combined a tribute to the iconography of Merton, with the incorporation of furs in heraldic rep-

---

67 Ayers, p. 55.

68 Hargreaves-Mawdsley, p. 60.

69 Hargreaves-Mawdsley, p. 191.

70 Christianson, 'The Sussex BA and the Grey Amess', p. 4. He adds: 'The original Sussex BA hood was itself suppressed in 2004, but the fur of the small grey nylon squirrel remains very much in demand'—to which the present writer would append the admonition of Dame Edna Everage: 'The acrylic is a protected animal.'

71 Buxton and Gibson, p. 25.

72 Henry VIII, An Acte for Reformacyon of Excesse in Apparayle (Statutes of the Realm), reprinted in Franklyn, p. 213. For a modernized translation and further commentary, see Cox.

73 Cox, p. 42.

74 Atchley, p. 317; reprinted in Franklyn, pp. 138–39.

75 Atchley, p. 321; reprinted in Franklyn, p. 141.

resentation or allusion—not only for Sussex bachelors, but as the basis of his entire system. If this is accepted, then a further premise logically follows Prof. Christianson's hypothesis, one that precisely explains the otherwise eccentric blue and white striped MA hood derided by Shaw: this was an evocation of vair, a form of squirrel fur, not only much used to line cloaks, but always represented in heraldry as repeated tessellated patterns of Azure and Argent. Hargreaves-Mawdsley's simplified design of vertical stripes (one no doubt far easier to acquire in silk than the more familiar cup-shapes) nonetheless also has heraldic parallels, being especially prominent in arms of the German-Czech House of Schwarzenburg.

> The animal was bluey-grey upon the back and white underneath, and the whole skin was used. It will be readily seen that by sewing a number of these skins together a result is obtained of a series of cup-shaped figures, alternating bluey-grey and white.[76]

Not all the medieval glass at the College remains where it was sited initially, and some panels were later transferred to the great west window. Among them is the fragment of a scholar (almost certainly part of the original sequence in the transept) wearing a fur-lined hood, a blue tippet with white fur edging and a blue gown (Fig. 5). Blue was a frequent substitute in medieval glazing for black, the latter being non-translucent. Nonetheless, the fur and the contrasting colours as they appear must make the image a strong contender for additional influence—especially as the gown is believed to be the *cappa nigra*, meaning that the figure is indeed arrayed as a Master of Arts, the degree for which Hargreaves-Mawdsley's striped hood was intended.[77]

There is, of course, no reason to suppose that Hargreaves-Mawdsley's first thoughts were of fur squares. It seems much more likely that his system developed downwards from doctoral colours, or outwards from the idea of referencing vair. The arms of Merton College were also in gestation during the foundation's early years: the ground (background colour) would be gold, but was formerly silver. In this variant, as shown in stained glass from the Warden's Lodging (Argent three chevrons party per pale, the first and third Azure and Gules, the second Gules and Azure), Argent is represented by white glass: another familiar juxtaposition of adjacent blue (and red) 'stripes' and white. Most tellingly, the arms of the University of Sussex, designed by Franklyn's nemesis Anthony Wagner, combine West Sussex blue and East Sussex red (along with elements from the arms of Brighton) as an identical blue and red chevron—Azure and Gules, divided into two by a line down the middle—placed on a silver ground. We may therefore confidently assume that Hargreaves-Mawdsley had shared his interpretations with Wagner, thus verifying the conjectured associations drawn from Merton's glass. The windows also have other strong elements, as noted by Ayers:

> Heraldry also played a role in shaping contemporary expectations, perceptions and interpretations of colour, establishing a limited number of tinctures, including gold and silver, and two furs ... The Merton scheme included heraldry in the tracery and the recorded main lights of the east window, as well as in the pseudo-heraldic

---

76 Fox-Davies, p. 62. The smaller size of vair was known as Menu-vair, hence 'miniver'. The heraldic depiction of vair may take several forms, but Hargreaves-Mawdsley indicated his stripes were vertical, which is certainly the commonest orientation.

77 Ayers, Part 2, p. 343, pl. 26.

Fig. 5. Scholar in blue gown and fur-trimmed tippet, Merton College, Oxford (*c.* 1413–25).

Fig. 6. Evangelist in green robe, Merton College, Oxford (*c.* 1305–12).

Fig. 7. St James the Great, Merton College, Oxford (*c.* 1305–12).

borders of the side windows ... The increasing popularity of heraldic representation within sacred settings has been explored not only as evidence for the increasing assertiveness of the secular elite, but also as an appropriation of this code by the clerical order for its own purposes. At Merton, the heraldic analogy is revealing of potential meaning on several levels ... The brightly-coloured and fur-lined gowns of the scholars perhaps also invite comparison with the clothes of the armigerous ...[78]

Hargreaves-Mawdsley would have been fully aware of this history and symbolism, and his alighting on green or gamboge as doctoral colours may be seen in their contiguity on the principal Merton figures. For example, in the seventh window on the south side in the eastern arm of the Chapel, sited prominently between two portraits of scholars in sober *cappa clausa*, is an image of a learned Evangelist in a yellow robe and striking green (Vert) mantle (Fig. 6)[79], presented as an intimate part of the community, in hierarchical collegiality. On the north side, a figure thought to be St Matthias is dressed identically, while St Thomas on the south side is garbed in similar fashion, but in gold mantle and blue-green tunic—perhaps the 'blue lights' referred to above. St Laurence has a yellow dalmatic, St Stephen a green one, and St James the Great wears a ruby tunic with a yellow mantle, as well as a broad-brimmed green 'bowler' hat—actually, a pilgrim's *galeno*, green denoting a bishop—the most likely source of the headgear scorned by Shaw. None of the kneeling supplicants are arrayed in these two colours: in addition to white and blue, they are most frequently clothed in scarlet and murrey, possible inspirations for the initial design for the vice-chancellor or the other doctorates. Yellow or gold evokes Venetian tradition, as well as heraldic Erminois (gold field with black spots). In closing these theories, it must be noted that the colours of the one original heraldic fur now remaining to Hargreaves-Mawdsley—white and black of ermine in various forms—would explain his second choice for the vice-chancellor: an off-white robe and black velvet cape (see below). This may recall the heavily-trimmed cope descended from the *cappa clausa* worn by the vice-chancellor at Cambridge when conferring degrees—or, a little less splendidly, the white furred hood of Oxford proctors. The chancellor was allocated a traditional black robe trimmed with gold braid; but, within the present parameters, even this might be construed as a nod to the ermine variant Pean (Or spots on a field Sable).

The very occasional use of green for genuine academic dress has also been noted by Prof. Christianson.[80] In the course of his investigation, he identifies several documents that mention it, particularly the will of one Richard Browne/Broune of Oxford, dated 8 October 1452, of which he quotes the translation: 'I bequeath to Master John Beke, Professor of Divinity, [...] a long green dress robe, together with a habit and hood of the same colour, lined with "miniver".' Hargreaves-Mawdsley makes no specific allusion to Browne's will in his volume, but he lists Robinson's paper in the bibliography, as well as citing it when referring to the colours of the Faculty of Canon Law at Salamanca

---

78 Ayers, p. 28.

79 A larger image showing the three figures is available at <docbrown.info/docspics /southwest/OxfordTrip/swspage09d.htm> [retrieved 19 July 2023].

80 Christianson, 'Doctors' Greens'. In modern times the colour is largely confined to the University of Leeds; however, St Andrews and Queen Margaret University, Edinburgh, both prescribe green robes for certain doctorates (determined by faculty colour rather than title of degree) and the MBA of Henley Business School is awarded a green gown with facings piped in old gold.

as red or crimson and green.[81] This is also noted by Edwin Clark, who comments, 'The green Gown is odd, and may throw some light on one or two curious costumes on our East Anglian screens'.[82] Green was a comparatively rare colour in medieval heraldry because the requisite ingredients, such as verdigris, did not produce long-lasting dyes.

In summary, Hargreaves-Mawdsley's initial scheme for Sussex, together with its posited associations, was as it appears in Table 1.

If this was indeed the basis of Hargreaves-Mawdsley's system, it possessed a piquant air of antiquity, in delightful contrast to the contemporary nature of the foundation for which it was designed. It must be admitted that some of the above associations are a little tenuous: miniver is 'a loose term ... Marten's fur was often used'.[83] A certain progressive logic is nonetheless evident: it may be observed that bachelors were allocated either grey or tawny from the colours of miniver, while masters flourished both in a more sophisticated design. While a radical departure from traditional academic dress, this is certainly not as piecemeal as its critics considered.

Franklyn also regarded himself as an expert in heraldry,[84] but if he deduced any such connections here—there is no indication that he did—he would surely have scorned the whole notion as a highly questionable, not to say fantastical, peg on which to hang a system of dress. By autumn, he could contain himself no longer. Convinced that the long-awaited demonstration was overdue (though it had still not been promised in the first place), he scribbled his ultimate postcard to Fulton's secretary.

> 24 September 1962
>
> I have heard NIL from you since 17th April & the promised demonstration has not come! So you have kept me at bay for a whole year now! Since many of the items of so-called academical dress have been approved and are being made (I know where, by whom, and most of the facts, very great calamity, a disaster), would you please send me a typed copy or printed copy of the present regulations, or of the descriptions of these strange garments. Strange that you did not ask me to be present at the meeting next Monday, altho' a morning is frequently impossible for a physician.
>
> Yours sincerely, Charles Franklyn

Ipse dixit. It is scarcely surprising that no reply was forthcoming; and thus Franklyn's turbulent communications with the University skidded to their ungracious expiration. He never forgave Sussex for the supposed slight; yet it is extraordinary how closely the whole futile saga would soon be resurrected with the universities of Essex and Warwick, as Franklyn's repackaged phrases, recycled speeches and embittered situations replayed themselves, spiralling ineluctably towards his dazzling coveted prizes, as a moth circles a lamp.

Establishing identity

A service was held at St Peter's Church, Brighton, on 21 October 1962 to inaugurate the University year. It had been proposed that full academic dress be worn by all who possessed it, although this was quickly amended to just those participating in the academ-

---

81 Hargreaves-Mawdsley, p. 26. The will is discussed in Robinson, p. 195.

82 Clark, p. 149; reprinted in Franklyn, p. 33. In the third part of his paper, Clark refers to the screen of Cawston Church, Norfolk, in this regard.

83 Hargreaves-Mawdsley, p. 193.

84 He revised Fox-Davies's seminal volume (see References) for six of its reprints from 1949.

Table 1. Speculative heraldic influences on Hargreaves-Mawdsley's scheme of academic dress for Sussex

Degree or official	Colours	Heraldic parallel	
Chancellor	Black and gold	Ermine / Pean	
Vice-Chancellor	White / Black (originally proposed as murrey and scarlet)	Ermine	
Higher (?) doctors	Yellow / Gamboge / Gold	Or, possibly Erminois	
Doctors	Green or blue	Vert or Azure	
Masters	Blue and white	Vair	
Bachelors	Grey or tawny (depending on faculty)	'Miniver', possibly marten or squirrel	

ic procession, i.e., the staff.[85] In the meantime, many Sussex undergraduates were keen to learn of the new proposals for their own gowns, and requested sight of materials and drawings.[86] Their enthusiasm was by no means universal. At the very first meeting of the Junior Common Room, before any academic dress for them had been decided, the students voted against wearing gowns, terming them 'archaic status symbols'.[87]

Monckton was also in discussion regarding his chancellor's robe, uncertain about the ecclesiastical connotations of a 'biretta' as approved by Ede & Ravenscroft, and rather preferring a square cap, an option that Hargreaves-Mawdsley was most anxious to avoid. The tall *pileus rotundus* would eventually be chosen, becoming one of the most characteristic features of the University's academic dress. Hargreaves-Mawdsley glosses 'biretta' as referring to both the 'horned and rigid variety of *pileus*;'[88] and *pileus* as 'used of the round cap in its various stages of development before its squareness appeared in the sixteenth century'.[89] At some point, he evidently modified this into the 'hard black domed biretta' referred to above, although the cap with a small stalk, which would become the sign of the doctorate, is worn by all the kneeling Merton scholars.

Discussions now broadened. Following the rejection of Wippell & Co., the advice of other firms was sought, including Cobleys, a leading outfitter of the time, who had several branches in the area. West Cumberland Silk Mills stated that their own silks

85 SxUOS1/2/31. Memos from A. E. Shields to invitees, 4 October 1962, 17 October 1962.
86 SxUOS1/1/1/17/24. Letter from Corbett to Fulton, 2 November 1962.
87 *Observer*, 8 October 1961.
88 Hargreaves-Mawdsley, p. 190.
89 Ibid., p. 194.

were unsuitable for robes, but George Cobley announced a range of hand-woven silks from Thailand and a prototype robe 'in the Marigold shade ... which should demonstrate how much more effectively the colours are highlighted by comparison with a small pattern of material ... From an aesthetic point of view the advice of a well-known artist would be helpful but only if combined with a practical knowledge of materials.'[90]

John Piper and the University

Hargreaves-Mawdsley, already fractious from committee interference, would certainly not have welcomed this suggestion or any further filtering of his ideas. Whatever discussion was held, the obvious first choice of creative mentor was approached at once, since 'anybody who hadn't heard of [John Piper] was a complete fool.'[91] One of the most versatile, innovative, and accomplished craftsmen of his time, Piper worked with great skill and beauty across nearly all media: painting, screen-printing, ceramics, fabrics, stained glass, photography, fireworks, and theatre design, including the premieres of most of Britten's operas. In conjunction with Patrick Reyntiens, he had just completed the magnificent Baptistery window for the new Coventry Cathedral, together with sets of vestments. A request was swift: 'Dr W. N. Hargreaves-Mawdsley ... has produced designs for the robes, and we are now at the stage of working out details of the colours and materials which are to be used. Mr Sekers, of West Cumberland Silk Mills, has promised his co-operation as far as materials are concerned, and we should very much appreciate it if you were willing (of course with an appropriate fee) to work in conjunction with him, and Dr Hargreaves-Mawdsley in the selection of the colours.'[92] A working lunch on 12 December at the Athenaeum was speedily arranged, once a further letter had clarified matters: 'Hargreaves-Mawdsley ... whom we invited nearly a year ago to think about *designs* of our robes ... is very anxious to break away from some of the nineteenth century English traditions (the mortarboard, for example). He has produced sketches for us based instead upon the Venetian tradition of academic dress. He also made suggestions about colours, but we have made little or no progress on colour. It is at this stage, when colour becomes an important issue, that I hoped that you would give us some help and advice, i.e., primarily on colours, though the line between design and colour must be somewhat flexible and by no means all the decisions on design have been irrevocably taken ... But it seems to me of paramount importance that *good* colours should be chosen. This is not only intrinsically important but also we have to bear in mind that we are leaving a legacy of colour (in such matters it is practically unchangeable) for an exceedingly long time ahead.'[93]

This is the first-known declaration of Venetian influence in connection with Sussex, but the basis for such a precise assertion has not been explored until now. Hargreaves-Mawdsley makes scant direct reference to the city in his volume, but does allude to the upright collar of the fifteenth-century robes of Doctors of Law and Medicine, as illustrated in the woodcuts of Francesco Vecellio (*c.* 1475–1560), a de-

90 SxUOS1/1/1/17/24. Letter from Cobley to Fulton, 5 November 1962.
91 Stained-glass artist Patrick Reyntiens, interviewed in *An Empty Stage: John Piper's Romantic Vision of Spirit, Place and Time.* Goldmark Films, 2010.
92 SxUOS1/1/1/17/24. Letter from Fulton to Piper (unsigned carbon copy), 16 November 1962.
93 SxUOS1/1/1/17/24. Letter from Fulton to Piper (unsigned carbon copy), 30 November 1962.

sign reflected in the high collars of doctors and officials at Sussex. Wide-open sleeves were also reserved especially for Venetian doctors of medicine (along with the doge and procurators), and although this style was not, of course, confined to Venice alone, Hargreaves-Mawdsley continued his unorthodoxy by choosing the sleeves of a master's gown for his doctors instead. The doctoral ribbons would appear to derive from the (usually scarlet) *becho* ('bird's beak'), a badge of office worn by Venetian gentlemen and citizens, defined as 'a long band of material, usually about 25 centimetres wide, worn, almost invariably, over the left shoulder.'[94] As with the epitoge, its derivation from what was essentially the liripipe of a large rolled hood, from which it had become detached over the years, would explain the absence of a doctoral hood in Hargreaves-Mawdsley's scheme. A similar decoration adorns the modern-day rector's gown at the University College of Economics and Commerce, Venice: 'From the left shoulder there hangs down, back and front, a red scarf embroidered with a design in gold thread and the lion of St. Mark—emblem of the city of Venice—and ending in two gold tassels.'[95] In addition, the rector wears an ermine cape, very similar to an almuce. Further influence may be traced to 'the most sumptuous of all the fabrics allowed to Venetians ... cloth of gold, often in the form of *restagno d'oro*, a patterned brocade woven entirely with a gold weft, though a plain unpatterned cloth of gold was worn too.'[96]

Piper replied by return, having been worried about too much involvement with too little time—'I found the vestments at Coventry involved so many difficult side-questions (and are still doing so) that I was not really competent to deal with the whole affair single handed'[97]—but was now agreeable to his lighter role. Unfortunately, the registrar's invitation to Hargreaves-Mawdsley did not reach him until after the meeting had taken place. This was quite possibly the first time the designer had been informed of Piper's co-opting, and proved to be the last straw: 'I never expected—nor, no doubt, did you expect—that this affair would drag on so long. Frankly, I have been most irritated by the attitude of the committee who have interfered with my proposals. I have given up enough of my time already. If the matter had been left in the hands of Mr Cobley and myself the whole system would have been drawn up and the robes made up long ago, but nowadays there must be committees for everything!'[98] Shields' reply was earnestly cordial, but his report of the lunch that had taken place without the designer, plus his proposals of yet further consulting and quibbling, must have done nothing to quell Hargreaves-Mawdsley's vexations. He was also unable to attend when Fulton, Piper and Sekers met for a second time at the Athenaeum on 7 January, during which Sekers' offer to provide fabrics for doctors' robes was gratefully accepted.[99] 'I think we are most

94 Newton, p. 12. There are also a few contemporary images showing the ribbon on the right shoulder, where Hargreaves-Mawdsley placed it. In the current system at Sussex, certain awards sport a ribbon on each shoulder.

95 Smith and Sheard, p. 1188.

96 Newton, p. 16.

97 SxUOS1/1/1/17/24. Letter from Piper to Fulton, 4 December 1962.

98 SxUOS1/1/1/17/24. Letter from Hargreaves-Mawdsley to Shields, 13 December 1962. It was ironic that the individual who had continually urged for the formation of a committee was, of course, Franklyn.

99 'Mr. N. Sekers presented a considerable quantity of shantung silk for the purpose of making up the academic robes worn by the Vice-Chancellor and the honorary graduates at the Installation of the Chancellor. Cobleys Ltd. made up the above-mentioned academic robes free

fortunate to have guidance from John Piper and from yourself,' Fulton remarked sanguinely, 'and I am sure that the upshot will be something very splendid and memorable.'[100] These arrangements were reported twice in the *Sunday Telegraph*:

> Brighton Belles
>
> John Piper, I hear, is helping to choose the colours of academic robes for the new university of Brighton. He hopes it will be his most spectacular display since he designed the décor and costumes for Britten's opera *Gloriana*.[101] Mr Norman Hargreaves-Mawdsley, an authority on academic dress, will be responsible for the robes themselves. And Mr Miki Sekers, the silk manufacturer, has offered to weave those worn by the honorary graduands at the installation of the Chancellor in June. Lord Monckton, first holder of the office, is, I am assured, delighted by all this interest and generosity—but is said to jib at an academic cap resembling a biretta.[102]

> Brighton Line
>
> Academic robes designed specially for the University of Sussex by Dr Norman Hargreaves-Mawdsley, with advice on dyes from John Piper, will be worn for the first time when Lord Monckton is installed as Chancellor on June 11 ... [Hargreaves-Mawdsley's] designs make a break with the tradition of most modern universities, which is to copy the dress of Oxford and Cambridge. Many of his ideas come from Europe—particularly Italy and France. Doctoral scarlet has been abandoned. This colour was adopted by Oxford and Cambridge after 1538 and was originally granted by papal authority to Bologna and Paris in the 14th century. Lord Monckton's Chancellor's robe and cap are more or less traditional, but the Vice-Chancellor, Mr J. S. Fulton, will wear white.[103]

Notwithstanding these accounts, Piper's involvement continued to be misinterpreted, but may now be fully assessed, and misconceptions corrected. It was not until 5 October 1963 that he was approached, rather apologetically, about the question of a fee; but, in fact, there was little Paying of the Piper. No further correspondence from the artist has been traced, nor does his name appear on the various committees convened to debate academic dress. This has not prevented some red herrings thriving in muddied waters, such as John Birch's visit to Piper's studio, where he allegedly saw 'some pieces of silk, samples for the new Doctors Robes he was designing for the University of Sussex.'[104] Piper's involvement ended before the silks in question had been procured by Cobleys, so if he did receive samples afterwards, it would have been for approval or interest only. Clarissa Lewis, Piper's daughter, is also adamant: 'I have no recollection of John doing any academic dress for Sussex. He did of course design vestments for Coventry and Chichester Cathedrals and I think others; so maybe John Birch might

---

of charge.' SxUOS1/1/1–GB181. Fourth Annual Report, 1962–63, p. 35.

100 SxUOS1/1/1/17/24. Letter from Fulton to Sekers, 9 January 1963.

101 First performed at the Royal Opera House, Covent Garden, 8 June 1953.

102 *Sunday Telegraph*, 10 February 1963.

103 *Sunday Telegraph*, 19 May 1963. The mention of 1538 is perhaps a reference to a ruling of a few years earlier: 'Henry VIII's Act for the Reformation of Excess of Apparel (1533), which, while forcing all people of private standing to adopt a more sober dress, allowed those of position to use such a colour as scarlet, no doubt gave a stimulus to its use on the festal robe which Doctors of Divinity and other doctors were beginning to wear.' Hargreaves-Mawdsley, p. 66.

104 Birch, p. 13. He does not specify the date of his visit, but the context seems to point to the early 1960s.

have seen silk samples for them.'[105] It may therefore be confidently deduced that although Piper had been perfectly amenable to discourse colours over two pleasant lunches at a London club, that was the extent of his contribution.

As the mantles, dalmatics and copes for Coventry resembled brilliantly jewelled panels of stained glass in equally intense yellow silks sourced from West Cumberland Silk Mills, it is easy to see how confusion arose, and continued to arise. In 1964, John Butterworth, vice-chancellor of Warwick, was in correspondence with the Council of Industrial Design about the proposed scheme of his own new University, remarking, 'I know well, of course, the gowns which John Piper has designed for the Cathedral here … might it be a possibility to commission someone who had experience in theatrical designing, but one would obviously have to be very careful not to become too flamboyant, as in my view are the robes at Sussex University.'[106] On 5 May, in a similarly-themed letter to Elizabeth Deighton of the Bear Lane Gallery in Oxford, Butterworth persisted in confusing and conflating the facts: 'I am a bit doubtful about John Piper who did the robes for Coventry Cathedral and the gowns for Sussex. I think they are tremendous as sketches but somehow to me don't quite come off when translated into material.'[107] If Butterworth had seen drawings by Piper, they too were most probably designs for Coventry; in any case, Piper was scrupulously careful across all his wide-ranging work to ensure that designs translated to other media would match his intentions accurately.

On 16 July 1974, the University conferred an honorary DLitt on Piper (his third such honour, five more would follow), from which occasion the precise nature of his assistance may also be confirmed. The programme stated that he would be presented by Quentin Bell, Professor of History and Theory of Art; but for some reason the duty was delegated to Donald Mitchell, founding Professor of Music and for many years the dominant force of the inner circle around Britten. His tribute to Piper, afterwards published in a limited-edition Festschrift, included a courtesy quote from Bell, then drew attention to the artist's long collaboration with the composer—most recently his designs for *Death in Venice*[108]—and after referring also to his work at Coventry, continued:

> … and to turn for a moment from the sublime to the domestic, it was from Mr Piper that this University sought advice when considering how its graduands should be robed. We cannot in fact quite claim that Mr Piper stands before us on this happy occasion wearing, as it were invisibly, a caption associated with a familiar if somewhat different category of artist: 'all my own work.' None the less there can be no doubt that the radiance and richness of the robes' colours reflect his influence and glowing imagination.[109]

Piper's definitive biography makes no mention of Sussex, other than to record the awarding of his honorary doctorate;[110] but soon afterwards he was commissioned to design a tapestry for its new interdenominational Chapel—known as the Meeting House, or, colloquially, the Beehive—interpreting scenes from Psalm 46, from which

105   Clarissa Lewis, email to author, 8 November 2022.
106   Quoted in Jackson, 'Warwick', p. 17.
107   Jackson, 'Warwick', pp. 18, 36.
108   First performed at Snape Maltings Concert Hall, Suffolk, 16 June 1973.
109   Elborn, pp. 76–77.
110   Spalding.

came the University's motto, Be still and know.[111] This building, where John Birch was the first Organist from 1967 to 1994, was dedicated at a brief service of thanksgiving on 15 December 1978, preceding the Seventeenth Annual Meeting of Court.

Similar myths, quickly established and long enduring, concerned Hardy Amies. An article in the *Daily Telegraph* on the scheme for the University of Essex, announced quite plainly that 'Mr Hardy Amies, the Queen's couturier, is designing the robes for the officers and graduates of the University of Essex. It is the first time he has designed academic dress of this kind'[112]—but his name was frequently cited incorrectly:

> How far we are from adapting our educational system to the demands of a techno-logical century was reflected in a singular ceremony which recently took place in Brighton. The occasion was the ceremony of conferring degrees at the university on recipients, who included Mr. Wilson, garbed in furred, saffron-yellow academic dress designed by Hardy Amies, and looking like a male chorus from Gilbert and Sullivan … if indeed so new and mini-skirted an institution still clings to the aca-demic mumbo-jumbo of the past … where indeed are we to look for salvation?[113]

… and—

> This tension for Plateglass between the pulls of a historic past and a beckoning future can be illustrated in a number of ways … They use gowns for their ceremo-nies, but have them designed by Cecil Beaton (the blue cape and tricorn hat of East Anglia) or Hardy Amies (Sussex and Essex), a peculiar mixture of high culture and haute couture.[114]

The lingering misattribution would not be easily shed. Len Brown, of Joshua Taylor, is also reported as having worked with Amies on the Sussex robes[115] but this cannot now be substantiated; it is most probable that either Brown's contact was Hargreaves-Mawd-sley, or he meant to refer to the University of Essex. Even by 2008, an enquiry by Alex Kerr to the Sussex archives[116] elicited an informal reply about designs 'which I think were for the Officers gowns where Sir Hardy Amies had been involved.'[117] No further response was received from Dr Kerr's source, and no evidence has been unearthed to confirm any contribution whatsoever by Amies. The legend that he was responsible for the bizarre scheme adopted by the University of Kent has also now been disproved.[118] In settling these claims, it is amusing to note a similarly prevalent but equally errone-ous belief among Sussex alumni that Basil Spence,[119] in an uncharacteristic display of

---

111　The tapestry, incorporating Piper's favoured 'foliate head', has 'proved to be an endur-ingly imaginative and striking piece of art.' Gavin Ashenden, 'The Meeting House' in Gray, p. 65.

112　*Daily Telegraph*, 7 January 1964

113　Beloff (p. 160) quotes this from Goronwy Rees (1909–79) in *Encounter* (Sept. 1966), p. 43, but erroneously ascribes it to the July issue. The description of a 'furred' gown is, in any case, entirely fictional.

114　Beloff, p. 186.

115　Goff, p. 12.

116　In connection with his article published later that year.

117　Email from Phyllis Hicks to Alex Kerr, 7 May 2008. The author is grateful to Dr Kerr for providing a copy of this communication.

118　Brewer, p. 12. Ede & Ravenscroft claimed authorship of the Kent scheme: Campbell, p. 108.

119　The architect of Sussex University, whose striking conception placed it among the

Voysey-esque comprehensiveness, had also designed the University's cutlery—resulting in quantities of relatively cheap kitchenware being hungrily purloined under false assumptions.[120] Many more misunderstandings and debates would occur before the academic dress of Sussex reached its final form.

Acknowledgements

My especial thanks to Rose Lock and the staff of The Keep, Brighton, who allowed me unrestricted access to a wealth of material and answered my questions with patience. Chloe Ratcliffe Schofield and her team at the University of Sussex checked a substantial number of other files, both physical and digital, that are inaccessible to the public: their discoveries have been few but invaluable, and my gratitude to them for a great deal of spade work on stony ground is not lessened because of the size of the harvest. The resources of the British Library, and the London Library and its staff, have been as indispensable as ever. I am particularly grateful to the late Dr Nicholas Groves, who shared with me his own earlier independent elucidation of the joint scheme between Shaw and Franklyn (thus complementing several of my own conclusions), but sadly died while this study was in preparation. In addition, I offer my gratitude to Prof. Tim Ayers (University of York), Dr Jonathan Cooper, the Revd Philip Goff, Dr Nicholas Jackson, Dr Alex Kerr, Dr Jane Mackay, James Middleton (Ede & Ravenscroft), Clarissa Lewis, Damien Ransome, Stuart Robinson, Dr Joseph Spooner, Dr Julia Walworth (Merton College, Oxford), Chris Williams, and Prof. Stephen Wolgast.

The author is grateful to the late Dr Groves for supplying the image in Figure 2; photographer unascertained. Chris Williams took the photograph from the Burgon Society Archive. Many thanks to Historic England for Figures 6 and 7.

All quotations from the writings and publications of George Shaw appear by kind permission of the Burgon Society.

All attempts to contact the copyright holder of Charles Franklyn have been unsuccessful.

References

Primary Sources

The Burgon Society: Letters and papers connected with George Shaw: Shaw: 1.1.1.6; 3.2 (1); 4.1.7

University of Sussex Collection, University of Sussex Special Collections at The Keep. Academic Dress June 1961–Oct 1966, SxUOS1/1/1/17/24

This file includes most of the quoted correspondence by Franklyn and Shaw, including the images reproduced as Figs 1A and 1E. Other sources held at The Keep that have been consulted are:

---

finest examples of modern university architecture. In 1970 the designs were considered for inclusion in a set of commemorative postage stamps. Unfortunately, the designs of the artist eventually chosen (Nicholas Jenkins) had not encompassed Sussex, so the set comprised representations of Southampton (for which Spence had also been partly responsible), Aberystwyth, Essex, and Leicester.

120 Spence also designed much of the furniture for the University Library and elsewhere, but his contribution to the cutlery was confined to the mere recommendation of a design by Gerald Benney for Viners of Sheffield. See Ann Eatwell, 'Early University Dining Culture' in Gray, pp. 137–38.

SxUOS1/1/2/32/2 Minutes of Court

SxUOS1/1/2/27/3/1-14 (Senate Meetings Minute Books)

SxUOS1/1/1/1–GB181 (Annual Reports)

S/224/13 Executive Summary of Business for Senate

SWG/1/1 and SWG/1/2 Senate Working Group on Academical Dress

SxMs59/6 (papers of W. G. Stone): Proposal of the University of Sussex and correspondence/reports 1955–62

Secondary Sources

Articles

Atchley, E. G. Cuthbert F., 'The Hood as an Ornament of the Minister at the Time of his Ministrations in Quire and Elsewhere', *Transactions of St Paul's Ecclesiological Society*, 4.5, (1900,), pp. 313–28; reprinted in Franklyn, pp. 136–45.

Baker, Richard, 'The Academic Dress of the University of Hull from 1954 to the Present Day, Including the Hull–York Medical School from 2003', *TBS*, 11 (2011), pp. 30–58.

Birch, John, 'Burgon: A Hooded Progress', *Burgon Society Annual 2002*, pp. 12–14.

Brewer, Michael H. L., 'Academic Dress in Canterbury', *TBS*, 11 (2011), pp. 8–29.

Christianson, Bruce, 'Doctors' Greens', *TBS*, 6 (2006), pp. 44–48.

—— 'The Sussex BA and the Grey Amess', *Burgon Notes*, 50 (Winter 2019/20), pp. 4–5.

Clark, E. C., 'English Academical Costume (Mediaeval)', *Archaeological Journal*, 50 (1893), pp. 73–104, 137–49, and 183–209; reprinted in Franklyn, pp. 11–47.

Cox, Noel, 'Tudor Sumptuary Laws and Academical Dress: An Act against Wearing of Costly Apparel 1509 and An Act for Reformation of Excess in Apparel 1533', *TBS*, 6 (2006), pp. 15–43.

Eggleston, Edmund, 'The Academic Dress of the University of Essex', *TBS*, 17 (2017), pp. 13–38.

Goff, Philip, 'Len Brown 1918–2007', *TBS*, 6 (2006), pp. 12–13.

Jackson, Nicholas, 'The Development of the Academic Dress in the University of Warwick', *TBS*, 8 (2008), pp. 10–59.

Kerr, Alex, and Shaw, Mary, 'George Wenham Shaw', *TBS*, 6 (2006), pp. 8–11.

Kerr, Alex, 'Hargreaves-Mawdsley's *History of Academical Dress* and the Pictorial Evidence for Great Britain and Ireland: Notes and Corrections', *TBS*, 8 (2008), pp. 106–50.

Ripley, Edward, 'Academic Dress of the University of Bath 1966–2020', *TBS*, 22 (2022), pp. 125–44.

Robinson, N. F., 'The Black Chimere of Anglican Prelates: A Plea for its Retention and Proper Use', *Transactions of the St Paul's Ecclesiological Society*, 4.3 (1898), pp. 181–220.

Scott, Elizabeth, 'The BCC Numbering System: Back to the Future?', *TBS*, 5 (2005), pp. 90–120.

Books

Ayers, Tim, *The Medieval Stained Glass of Merton College, Oxford, Corpus Vitrearum Medii Aevi VI* (Oxford: OUP, 2013).

Beloff, Michael, *The Plateglass Universities* (London: Secker & Warburg, 1968).

Buxton, L. H. Dudley, and Gibson, Strickland, *Oxford University Ceremonies* (Oxford: OUP, 1935).

Campbell, Una, *Robes of the Realm: 300 Years of Ceremonial Dress* (London: Ede & Ravenscroft, 1989).

Daiches, David (ed.), *The Idea of a New University: An Experiment in Sussex* (London: Andre Deutsch, 1964).

Elborn, Geoffrey (ed.), *To John Piper on his Eightieth Birthday: 13 December 1983* (London: Stourton Press, 1983).

Fox-Davies, A. C., *A Complete Guide to Heraldry* (London: Orbis Publishing, 1985).

Franklyn, Charles. A. H., *Academical Dress from the Middle Ages to the Present Day, Including Lambeth Degrees* (Lewes: W. E. Baxter, 1970).

Gray, Fred (ed.), *Making the Future: A History of the University of Sussex* (Brighton: University of Sussex, 2011).

Groves, Nicholas, *Charles Franklyn: A Man of Strong Opinions* (London: Burgon Society, 2022).

Hargreaves-Mawdsley, W. N., *A History of Academical Dress in Europe until the End of the Eighteenth Century* (Oxford: Clarendon Press, 1963).

Haycraft, Frank W., *The Degrees and Hoods of the World's Universities and Colleges*, 5th edn (Lewes: W. E. Baxter, 1972).

Humbert, Harold F., 'The Hampton Court Conference' (PhD thesis, University of Edinburgh, 1940).

Jackson, Nicholas (ed.), *Ackermann's Costumes of the Universities of Oxford and Cambridge*, Burgon Society Historical Reprints, 1 (London: Burgon Society, 2016).

Newton, Stella, *The Dress of the Venetians 1495–1525* (Aldershot: Scolar Press, 1988).

Shaw, George W., *Academical Dress of British Universities* (Cambridge: Heffer, 1966).

—— *Academical Dress of British and Irish Universities* (Chichester: Phillimore,1995).

Smith, Hugh, and Sheard, Kevin, *Academic Dress and Insignia of the World* (Cape Town: A. A. Balkema, 1970).

Spalding, Frances, *John Piper, Myfanwy Piper: Lives in Art* (Oxford: OUP, 2009).

Transactions of the Burgon Society, 23 (2023), pages 75–93

The History of Undergraduate Academical Dress in Britain's Modern Universities since 1880, with a Discussion of its Recent and Current Use

By Edward Teather

Abstract

Undergraduates in cap and gown are a sight associated today with a select few universities. Despite this, over thirty British universities prescribe academic dress for undergraduates. For many of the universities founded in the twentieth century, the adoption of undergraduate cap and gown was a part of establishing an *esprit de corps*. Some 1960s universities attempted radical reforms to undergraduate dress, which in some cases were rejected by students. Over the twentieth century undergraduate gowns faded from view; however, their current use is slightly broader than has been generally considered, thanks to a number of traditional halls of residence at civic universities.

S haw's *Academical Dress* shows us that, of the United Kingdom's roughly 170 universities and degree-awarding bodies, 33 currently prescribe academical dress for undergraduate students.[1] Despite this, undergraduates in cap and gown are a sight associated today with very few universities: matriculation and examinations at Oxford; the college formal dinners of Oxford, Cambridge and Durham; and the scarlet St Andrews undergraduate gown. These have been described as 'pockets of resistance' against the casualizing trends in university education; however, they represent only a small proportion of even those universities that prescribe undergraduate cap and gown.[2] Nearly thirty 'modern'[3] universities—that is to say, universities founded since the late nineteenth century—also either have undergraduate dress in their regulations or have done at some stage over the twentieth century. At the 'civic'[4] universities, un-

---

1   Nicholas Groves (ed.), *Shaw's Academical Dress of Great Britain and Ireland*, 3rd edn (London: Burgon Society, 2011–14), Vol. I (hereafter Shaw (2011)).

2   Oliver James Keenan, 'How Can Academical Dress Survive in the Third Millennium?', *TBS*, 10 (2010), pp. 99–125 (p. 105), doi.org/10.4148/2475-7799.1086.

3   This article does not consider any universities founded before 1880. This is a practical decision taken based on the different approaches to university education taken by universities following Manchester in foundation, and is not intended to make the claim that no university founded before that point could be considered modern.

4   I have defined the civic universities (a term used largely interchangeably with redbrick within this article and in some, but not all, other literature) as having been founded between Manchester (Victoria) in 1880 and 1960. Manchester is certainly the first redbrick university, and though London has been categorized as a civic, its foundation does not feature the notable collaboration between the city institutions and the growing college that preceded the grant of a royal charter. 1960 has been chosen for convenience as the beginning of a decade of university

dergraduate cap and gown were often adopted—whether from the Senate or through student movements—in order to foster a sense of *esprit de corps* that was seen as lacking from the new universities compared to Oxford and Cambridge (a topic of Truscot's *Red Brick University*).[5] The gowns adopted were of existing patterns and followed the conservative trends set largely at Cambridge or London. In many cases the wearing of academical dress on a day-to-day basis was not enforced, and even in some cases where enforcement nominally existed, the practice nevertheless seems to have generally fallen into disuse. The 1960s saw radical change in British higher education,[6] and it is surprising that as many as twelve universities established since 1960 either currently or formerly prescribed academic dress for undergraduates. The designs of gowns in this period sometimes differed radically from the norms established; however, in all cases they were short-lived experiments that do not seem to have seen any significant use since the end of the decade that introduced them. The ideals of *esprit de corps* and corporate life were drawn upon; however, cultural changes in the newer universities ensured that they were not as significant as they had been decades before. At many universities undergraduate cap and gown have become a historical obsolescence, remaining in regulations but largely unused, but at a few universities traditional or collegiate halls of residence have retained the use of undergraduate academical dress. Some universities have found other uses for undergraduate gowns. These are examples of strange traditions which appear anathema to the image of many modern universities but are traditions which ought to be noted.

'Esprit de corps': undergraduate dress of the civic universities (1880–1960)

Hargreaves-Mawdsley finished his history of academic dress with the end of the eighteenth century, dismissing the robemakers of the nineteenth as 'borrowing freely and without true knowledge of the manner whereby the old universities had gradually acquired their costume'.[7] Despite any number of petitions, the nineteenth century saw the establishment of only four universities in Great Britain (not including Ireland), and it was not until the early twentieth century that the university extension movement had gained significant traction to see the establishment of redbrick or civic colleges as universities. The adoption of academical dress for undergraduates at these universities was a piecemeal affair, though largely a restrained one. At Oxbridge, cap and gown were as much a symbol of discipline as pride, being an identifying mark for the proctors.[8] Though discipline could be a problem at the civics,[9] it was not on the

expansion although no new university was founded in that year.

5   Bruce Truscot, *Red Brick University* (London: Faber & Faber, 1943). William Whyte, *Somewhere to Live: Why British Students Study Away from Home—And Why it Matters*, HEPI Report 121 (Oxford: Higher Education Policy Institute, 2019), p. 19.

6   The plate-glass universities are considered those founded during the 1960s, particularly following the Robbins Report. I have not included a separate category for universities founded between 1969 and 1992 for the reason that none of them adopted undergraduate academical dress; and I have broadly included all 1960s universities under the plate-glass umbrella, again for simplicity.

7   W. N. Hargreaves-Mawdsley, *A History of Academical Dress in Europe until the End of the Eighteenth Century* (Oxford: Clarendon Press, 1963), p. vii.

8   Paul R. Deslandes, *Oxbridge Men: British Masculinity and the Undergraduate Experience, 1850–1920* (Bloomington: Indiana University Press, 2005), p. 103.

9   See Edward Fiddes, *Chapters in the History of Owens College and of Manchester Uni-*

Fig. 1. Caroline Chadwick wearing the Owens College (Manchester) undergraduate gown.

whole a force behind the adoption of academical costume, which was instead often driven by a perceived need to boost *esprit de corps* amongst a student body that spent its days in a markedly different manner from those living in colleges at Oxford or Cambridge.

Owens College, a predecessor to the University of Manchester, was the first of the civics by a generation, and pioneered of a new sort of university education.[10] When academical dress was discussed during the nineteenth century it was ruled that there would be none for undergraduates.[11] The earliest student petition for academical dress came in 1854; however, 'the authorities deemed it inadvisable to allow the wearing of a costume so incongruous with the squalid surroundings of the college.'[12] In 1880

versity, 1851–1914 (Manchester: Manchester University Press, 1937), p. 116; J. C. Holt, *The University of Reading: The First Fifty Years* (Reading: Reading University Press, 1977), p. 6. Both show poor discipline as a reason for establishing halls of residence at their respective universities.

10 Alex Robertson and Colin Lees, 'Owens College and the Victoria University, 1851–1903', in Brian S. Pullan (ed.), *A Portrait of the University of Manchester* (London: Third Millennium Publishing, 2007), pp. 10–16 (p. 11).

11 Philip Lowe, 'The Origins and Development of Academical Dress at the Victoria University of Manchester', *Burgon Society Annual 2001*, pp. 25–32 (p. 25), doi.org/10.4148/2475-7799.1004.

12 Owens College, *Record of the Jubilee Celebrations at Owens College, Manchester* (Man-

the Victoria University was created as a federal institution for the north of England. Life at the new university did not feature the formalities of undergraduate life at Oxbridge or Durham, and so the academic costume committee again did not recommend undergraduate dress, which caused student protest. An anonymous student wrote to a newspaper 'to express some little astonishment at the absence of some academic costume for the Victoria undergraduates',[13] highlighting that London undergraduates were entitled to a gown. There was some encouragement of undergraduate academical dress at Owens during the 1870s and 1880s, and Lowe speculates that this was in part due to college principal Joseph Greenwood, in whose handwriting an amendment to the calendar inviting undergraduates of any university to wear the dress to which they were entitled appears.[14] It should be noted that Greenwood was also a supporter of the residential aspect of the College,[15] and that he could have seen these aspects of tradition, which as Lowe mentions he would have known from his time at Cambridge, as two sides of the same coin. Despite this, the undergraduates of the Victoria University entered the twentieth century in plain clothes.

Outside changes to London regulations it seems the only new undergraduate dress adopted in the late nineteenth century was that used by the then University of Wales College, Aberystwyth (now the University of Aberystwyth), which used 'the Oxford scholar, but the sleeves gathered (like London BA) with green cords and buttons'.[16] A student wrote in the late nineteenth century that the cap and gown were required 'all the while and everywhere' though oddly 'except in chapel or our lodgings'[17]—these two places would later become the stalwarts of undergraduate gown-wearing at the civic universities, though here 'lodgings' likely refers to rented houses, or rooms within houses, rather than the more formal halls of residence.

The early years of the twentieth century saw newly chartered universities, and with them new regulations on undergraduate costume. In 1900 the new University of Birmingham adopted undergraduate cap and gown (the latter of the Birmingham pattern—an Oxford scholar's [u2] with the sleeve seam open—also used at Lampeter and Leicester).[18] At Manchester, authorities had been worn down and by the jubilee of 1902 'the days of probationary plain clothes [were] fulfilled, and the distinction of cap and gown conferred on undergraduates.'[19] The 'short-lived' Manchester gown was of an unknown design with open and deeply pleated sleeves (Figs 1, 2).[20]

chester: Sherratt & Hughes, 1902), p. 5. (Hereafter, *Record of the Jubilee.*)

13 *Evening Mail.* 30 April 1881. Quoted in Lowe (2001). p. 30.

14 Lowe (2001), pp. 25–26.

15 Colin Lees and Alex Robertson, 'Early Students and the "University of the Busy": The Quay Street Years of Owens College, 1851–1870', *Bulletin of the John Rylands Library*, 79 (1997), pp. 116–94 (p. 171).

16 William Gibson and Nicholas Groves, 'The Origins of the University of Wales Robes', *TBS*, 8 (2008), pp. 91–97 (p. 96), doi.org/10.4148/2475-7799.1064.

17 E. L. Ellis, *The University College of Wales, Aberystwyth, 1872–1972* (Cardiff: University of Wales Press, 1972), p. 48.

18 Thomas A. Goodman, 'The Academic Dress of the University of Birmingham' (2019) <www.researchgate.net/publication/334459727_The_Academic_Dress_of_the_University _of_Birmingham> [retrieved 6 February 2024].

19 *Record of the Jubilee*, p. 5.

20 Alex Kerr, 'The Turbulent History of Undergraduate Academical Dress, Summary of an

Fig. 2 (left). A student in the Owens College (Manchester) undergraduate gown, c. 1900.

Fig. 3 (right). A University of Manchester undergraduate gown, showing the cording on the yoke. It is no longer prescribed by the University but is worn in some halls.

The wearing of undergraduate dress at Manchester was a fervour of the jubilee year: by 1904 it was ridiculed in a student publication[21] and in 1919 it was removed from University regulations as 'obsolete'.[22] The association of gown-wearing with the jubilee of the College is significant, and the use of the phrase 'probationary plain clothes' in a University publication makes it clear that the conferring of gowns upon undergraduates somehow demonstrated the College coming of age as a university.[23] The adoption of gowns for the jubilee also demonstrates that academic dress in this period aimed to work alongside other initiatives such as students' unions, sports teams, and halls of residence, in promoting an image of university life and developing the *esprit de corps* that, it was considered in the nineteenth century, set the ancient universities apart from the new.[24] At Birmingham in the same year a student wrote that enforcing the wearing of gowns upon undergraduates would 'stamp all members [of the University] with what one might call a "Varsity stamp".'[25] A comparison was made to the University of Wales colleges, which all enforced gown-wearing.[26] Again the aim was to create a group identity for students. By 1940 this had moved from a mark of pride to a mark

Illustrated Talk by Alex Kerr, Burgon Society Study Day, 7 May 2011', *Burgon Notes*, 17 (Summer 2011), pp. 2–3. Also found, with a different image, at <www.scribd.com/document/65743270/Alex-Kerr-2011-Undergraduate-Academic-Dress#>.

21 Philip Lowe, *Manchester Academical Dress: A Guide and History* (Manchester: privately printed, 2002), pp. 23–24.

22 Lowe (2002), p. 28.

23 *Record of the Jubilee*, p. 5.

24 Gary S. Messinger, *Manchester in the Victorian Age: The Half-known City* (Manchester: Manchester University Press, 1985), p. 145.

25 Quoted in William Whyte, *Redbrick: A Social and Architectural History of Britain's Civic Universities* (Oxford: Oxford University Press, 2015), p. 147.

26 Ibid.

of difference, when the Students' Guild at Birmingham rejected a proposal to make gown-wearing at council meetings optional as 'it was a privilege which distinguished members of the University from students at the Technical College.'[27]

In 1909 the University of Bristol decided against the use of undergraduate gowns (as did Queen's University Belfast, around the same time),[28] but by 1911 had added gowns of the [u2] Oxford Scholars' pattern to its regulations.[29] A year later it was noted that these were worn 'on the very coldest of days, and then only to keep warm'.[30] Depending on the university, the impetus to wear academic dress might come from the Senate or from the student body, but it seemed at least a point of discussion at most of the civics. The University of Sheffield adopted an unspecified undergraduate gown in 1908,[31] which later became the [u2], along with Leeds. The lie of the land in 1909 was described by the University of Bristol Gown Committee, which reported that undergraduate dress was 'regularly worn [at] Cambridge, Oxford, Dublin, Durham and Newcastle, [Bangor, Cardiff, and] St Andrews'; worn by some students at Glasgow and Aberdeen; an option at Sheffield; and in use only for ceremony at London, Manchester, and Birmingham.[32] This report shows the range of undergraduate dress in British (and Irish) universities in this period. Whilst it suggests that Aberystwyth had ceased to use its gowns, satirical and photographic records of the 1920s show the College's students enrobed.[33] Reading added blue facings to a [u2] gown, marking the first case of chromatic departure in England (outside of Cambridge college variations), which would become common. Gowns seem to have been encouraged at Reading: in the 1920s and 30s one lecturer was known for reproving students who entered his classes without one,[34] and in 1921 regulations requested that 'women students going into the town should either wear cap and gown or ordinary costume.'[35] Pictorial evidence from the 1920s also suggests that gowns were in common usage among students for at least formal occasions.[36]

Another factor in the difference in use between Oxbridge and the civics was the presence of women. While the new universities remained predominantly male environments, they had begun admitting women students as full members earlier than Oxbridge.[37] Deslandes has portrayed cap and gown as a 'badge of manhood',[38] and the

27 E. W. Ives, *The First Civic University: Birmingham 1880–1980: An Introductory History* (Birmingham, University of Birmingham Press, 2000), p. 386.

28 G. W. Shaw, *Academical Dress of British Universities* (Cambridge: Heffer, 1966), p. 45.

29 Paul Hayward, 'Bristol Blue: A Search for the Origins of Academic Dress at the University of Bristol', *TBS*, 21 (2021), pp. 185–207 (p. 188), doi.org/10.4148/2475-7799.1201.

30 Quoted in Whyte (2015), p. 148.

31 Nicholas Gledhill, 'Academical Dress at the University of Sheffield: A Timeline', *TBS*, 4 (2004), pp. 49–52 (p. 49), doi.org/10.4148/2475-7799.1030.

32 Hayward, p. 199.

33 Geraint H. Jenkins, *The University of Wales: An Illustrated History* (Cardiff: University of Wales Press, 1993), p. 122.

34 Holt, p. 92.

35 Holt, p. 355.

36 Sidney Smith and Michael Bott, *One Hundred Years of University Education in Reading: A Pictorial History 1892–1992* (Reading: University of Reading Press, 1992), p. 50.

37 Oxford and Cambridge had women students but they were not matriculated members of the universities.

38 Deslandes, p. 104.

Burgon Society archives WBS-063 (f)
Fig. 4. University of Reading undergraduate gown.

Burgon Society Archives WBS-429 (f)
Fig. 5. University of Hull undergraduate gown.

Burgon Society archives WBS-204 (f)
Fig. 6. University of Leicester undergraduate gown. This pattern was also used at Birmingham and Lampeter.

warden of the women's hall at Manchester was against their adoption; however, when it came down to a student vote at Manchester in 1907, a greater proportion of women than men voted in favour of enforced academic dress.[39]

Some universities, as Manchester had before, adopted undergraduate dress before being granted full university status. Gowns had been enforced at the University College of Southampton in 1923, when the college principal drew on the idea of *esprit de corps* in asking students 'to look upon the cap and gown as the symbol of our corporate life'.[40] The enforcement of academic dress was unpopular, as some lines from a poem printed in a student magazine show:

> Now that the powers which sway our destinies
> Decree that we a sable robe must wear.
> In spite of all our cries and woeful pleas [...]
> Though some may 'swank' the undergraduate gown,
> Thank Heaven I need not wear it in the town.[41]

The University of Leicester adopted undergraduate dress while still a university college, choosing the Birmingham pattern: 'knee-length, with open forearm sleeves', and required students wear them in lectures.[42] At Nottingham a unique gown was designed for undergraduates before the grant of a royal charter in 1948, like Liverpool adopting a longer gown of bachelor's length and with what John Horton describes as

---

39 Lowe (2002), pp. 52, 25.

40 *Southampton University College Magazine*, 23 (59) (Easter 1923), p. 4.

41 Ibid., 23 (57), p. 39.

42 Clifford Dunkley, 'Academic Dress of the University of Leicester', *TBS*, 11 (2011), pp. 59–75 (p. 60), doi.org/10.4148/2475-7799.1092.

Fig. 7. A student in a Nottingham University undergraduate gown, photographed in the 1930s or 40s.

Fig. 8. An early ceremony at the University of Nottingham in 1948, featuring undergraduates in academic dress. Note the wide sleeves and the length of the gowns.

'open, wide and relatively short' sleeves of a bell shape. As at Manchester before, staff at the new University who had been at Oxbridge may have brought an idea of tradition and ceremony with them—Nottingham's first vice-chancellor, Bertrand Hallward, had been a proctor at Cambridge.[43] As these colleges became universities over the next few decades, their academic dress—and the attitude of their students towards it—changed.

In 1957 at the then University of Southampton 'the student newspaper called— once more—for the wearing of gowns to be made compulsory in order to create a cor- porate spirit.'[44] The London pattern [u3] gown was chosen. Upon becoming a uni- versity in 1957 Leicester reassessed its academical dress and with it adopted a new undergraduate gown. 'Guardsman' or 'Cardinal' red was considered—likely due to Scottish influence—however, the customary black was eventually chosen:[45] 'Oxford scholars' shape, with the forearm seam left open. The sleeves and back are ruched, but not pleated in the usual way.'[46]

As the later civics became universities they adopted undergraduate dress as a matter of course. At Hull, where the gowns were black with sky-blue facings and yoke, the specifications mandated 'Gowns ... for both staff and undergraduates at lectures,

---

43 The author would like to thank John Horton for the information provided about the University of Nottingham's undergraduate gown.

44 Whyte (2015), p. 242.

45 Dunkley, p. 61.

46 Shaw (1966), p. 70.

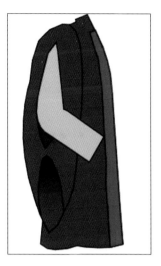

Burgon Society Archives (WBS-637 (f)

Burgon Society Archives (WBS-235 (f)

Fig. 9. University of Keele undergraduate gown. The [u3] pattern was also used at Southampton and (with red cording) at Manchester.

Fig. 10. University of Leeds undergraduate gown. The [u2] pattern was used widely at the civic universities, including Wales, Sheffield, and Bristol; and was adopted at some of the plate-glass universities in the 1960s.

Fig. 11. The University of Exeter Scholars' gown, based on illustrations in *Shaw* (1966).

written examinations, ceremonial occasions and official interviews'.[47] At Exeter undergraduates were required to be in academical dress for 'lectures, classes and tutorials, in chapel and when visiting members of the academic staff officially'.[48] The gown was a [u3], though with a separate scholars' gown featuring green facings and yoke: 'It is not known when [this] was introduced, nor if it is still current.'[49] The image of buying your gown as a part of the rite of passage associated with 'going up' was beginning to settle in to some of the new universities.

The most radical decisions in terms of undergraduate academic dress was at Liverpool, which prescribed a Cambridge MA gown for undergraduates, with cord and button on the yoke—considered a 'strange anomaly' by Shaw.[50] Liverpool was an outlier and the general trend was not one of great innovation; however, many of the redbrick universities—certainly the earlier foundations—clearly saw it as important that they adopt undergraduate dress as part of the trappings of becoming a university

47 See images WBS-429 (f) and WBS-429 (b), at <burgon.org.uk/archive/hull> [retrieved 28 April 2024]. Richard Baker, 'The Academic Dress of the University of Hull from 1954 to the Present Day, Including the Hull-York Medical School from 2003', *TBS*, 11 (2011), pp. 30–58 (p. 32), doi.org/10.4148/2475-7799.1091.

48 David C. Quy, 'An Overview of the History of the Academic Dress of the University of Exeter', *TBS*, 19 (2019), pp. 38–54 (p. 39), doi.org/10.4148/2475-7799.1163.

49 Shaw (2011), p. 178.

50 Shaw (1966), p. 5.

and developing traditions that would foster *esprit de corps*. For the most part in the modern universities it is evident that undergraduate academic dress has faded away, with change taking place at different speeds at different universities. At Bristol gowns are at least nominally enforced at lectures to this day, though are hardly to be seen (see section below), and by the 1920s were seen by students as an unnecessary emulation of Oxbridge;[51] whereas at Birmingham '[as] late as 1950 a survey … reported that students were generally in favour of academic dress', though rationing presented a problem. The pattern at Birmingham was a common one: 'Gowns were never abolished. They symbolized the old order, and they faded away.'[52]

Undergraduate dress at the plate-glass universities and beyond (1960–)

The Robbins Report saw the number of universities in the United Kingdom doubled, and the creation of new kinds of university. Some of the new 'plate-glass' universities had existed before as colleges and brought academic dress forward with them from their pre-university days (such as a 1902 student petition at what was then Loughborough University College, which succeeded in adopting undergraduate dress)[53] but others had been created anew and were imbued with a spirit of innovation. The rationale for adopting (and even enforcing in some cases) academical dress for undergraduates is not as evident as in the civic examples already discussed; however, in some cases the idea of promoting a unified corporate identity seems to have played a part.

Both the University of Sussex and the University of East Anglia were radical departures from the mock-gothic or redbrick norm in terms of their campuses, and complemented the gleaming white concrete of Bradbury's satire[54] with a pair of new undergraduate gowns ([u6] and [u7] respectively). At Sussex, a sleeveless gown was designed by academic dress historian Norman Hargreaves-Mawdsley and was considered a 'radical' departure, though Shaw 'said that some features of [the scheme] showed tendencies to return to the style of dress worn in the medieval universities of Europe.'[55] Within a week of going up to Sussex, the first cohort of undergraduates had ceased to wear the 'archaic status symbols' of their gowns.[56] Undergraduate gowns at Sussex may not have been a success, but in Norwich the gowns of the UEA caused a stir with its fashion. During its foundation, the UEA presented a vision of university life that was 'attractive to conservative rural Norfolk and Suffolk', and plans for halls of residence featured 'rather idealistic drawings of young men (not women) in residence, wearing ties, jackets and gowns, with firm clean-shaven jaws, earnestly reading'.[57] The undergraduate gowns, like the rest of the academic dress scheme, were designed by Cecil Beaton and first appeared in 1966. They followed the trends of colour-changing begun at Reading and Exeter with a

---

51 Whyte (2015), p. 182.

52 Ives, p. 387.

53 Whyte (2015), p. 153.

54 See Malcolm Bradbury, *The History Man* (London: Secker & Warburg, 1975).

55 Alex Kerr, 'Hargreaves-Mawdsley's *History of Academical Dress* and the Pictorial Evidence for Great Britain and Ireland: Notes and Corrections', *TBS*, 8 (2008), pp. 106–50 (p. 108), doi.org/10.4148/2475-7799.1066.

56 Fred Gray, *Making the Future: A History of the University of Sussex* (Falmer: University of Sussex, 2011), p. 101.

57 Michael Sanderson, *The History of the University of East Anglia, Norwich* (London: Hambledon & London, 2002), p. 51.

'smokey blue'[58] sleeveless gown with black facings.[59] A tricorn cap was initially included, but soon was replaced by the more usual square shape. *The Times* likened the UEA undergraduates in their gowns to the 'Mods', and a year later became a 'sixties fashion statement' when modelled by radio hostesses.[60] In the brave new world of the plate-glass universities, students no longer clamoured for a mark of status as they had at the civics at the turn of the century and as recently as 1957.

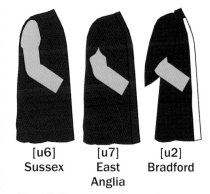

[u6]
Sussex

[u7]
East
Anglia

[u2]
Bradford

Fig. 12. Recent undergraduate gowns that demonstrate departures from the norm in both pattern and colour, based on illustrations in *Shaw* (1966, 2011).

In a similar vein the undergraduates of the University of Hertfordshire (notable as the only post-1992[61] university that prescribes undergraduate dress) are entitled to wear a London BA gown without a hood.[62] This decision was a more pragmatic one than those taken at Sussex or the UEA, the designers of Hertfordshire's academic costume deciding that: 'gowns were more likely to be worn if they were of a pattern ready to hand.'[63] Other recent universities may have a history of undergraduate academical dress, though there is no present use, for instance the University of Cumbria was formed in 2007 from the merging of the Cumbria Institute of the Arts and St Martin's College, Lancaster. The latter had 'initially' (during the 1960s) enrobed its students, to encourage high academic standards.[64]

Radical departures from the black stuff of the old universities would continue. The University of Lancaster required its early cohorts of students (until 1966) to wear a grey [u3] gown to lectures; and the University of Bradford (technically) enrobed its undergraduates in a maroon gown of the Oxford scholar's cut with silver facings.[65] Perhaps the most dramatic variations took place at the University of Dundee. Despite

58 Sanderson, p. 136.

59 University of East Anglia, 'Official and Academic Dress', Calendar <www.uea.ac.uk /about/university-information/university-governance/academic-calendar/official-and-academic-dress> [retrieved 6 February 2024].

60 Sanderson, p. 136.

61 The Further and Higher Education Act (1992) changed the UK higher education scene significantly by converting all polytechnics into universities. While 'post-1992' now generally refers to universities founded due to this Act and in the years that followed (i.e., not into the twenty-first century), the most recently founded university discussed is Hertfordshire (1992), and therefore any discrepancy in the definition 1992–present is irrelevant.

62 Shaw (2011), p. 204.

63 Bruce Christianson and Philip Waters, 'Reflections of Designing the Academic Dress of the University of Hertfordshire', *TBS*, 20 (2020), pp. 150–61 (p. 156), doi.org/10.4148/2475-7799.1183.

64 Peter S. Gedge and Lois M. R. Louden, *S. Martin's College, Lancaster, 1964–89* (Lancaster: Centre for North-West Regional Studies, University of Lancaster, 1989), p. 12.

65 Peter William Clarke, 'McKinlay's People: A Study of the Academic Dress of the University of Bradford', *TBS*, 16 (2016), pp. 13–29 (p. 25), asserts that 'it could be argued that [ceremonial usher's] gowns form the basis of the undergraduate academic dress of the University.' doi.org/10.4148/2475-7799.1138.

Burgon Society Archives WBS-070 (f)

Fig. 13. University of Lancaster undergraduate gown.

Burgon Society Archives (WBS-951 (f)

Fig. 14. University of Dundee undergraduate gown.

being a nominally modern university, the University of Dundee is considered an ancient one by law. In Scotland it 'is alone among the modern universities in sharing the tradition of the red undergraduate gown'.[66] In 1899 the Student Representative Council adopted the St Andrews gown for undergraduates (in 'appreciation' of the college becoming a part of that university)[67] but differentiated the Dundee gown by the addition of a pentagonal badge bearing a representation of lilies, made of the same material as the collar, on to the left breast. In 1954 this gown was replaced with a gown of the St Andrews cut in dark blue, though this would last only until university status was granted in 1967, when the undergraduate gown was restored to red, only with 'a yoke, collar and facings of serge or flannel in "Stewart blue"'.[68] This gown remains a part of university regulations.[69]

Other universities were more restrained. The University of Newcastle had begun its life as two colleges of the University of Durham, and continued the [u4] of that university into its own regulations when it gained university status of its own in 1963. The universities of Keele, Loughborough, and Bath adopted black gowns of existing patterns ([u3] for the former and [u2] for the latter two). The University of Strathclyde prescribes one of only two black undergraduate gowns in Scotland (the other being for divinity students at St Andrews), though with a blue button and cord.[70] It is also the newest Scottish university to have adopted academic dress for undergraduates.

66 , Jonathan C. Cooper, 'The Scarlet Gown: History and Development of Scottish Undergraduate Dress', *TBS*, 10 (2010), pp. 8–42 (p. 31). doi.org/10.4148/2475-7799.1082

67 Donald Southgate, *University Education in Dundee: A Centenary History* (Edinburgh: Edinburgh University Press, 1982), p. 143.

68 Cooper, pp. 31, 21.

69 The University of Dundee, 'Academic Dress of the University', 7 July 2023, at <www.dundee.ac.uk/guides/academic-dress-university> [retrieved 8 February 2024].

70 Cooper, p. 32.

For many of the new universities of the 1960s, academic dress was a part of form-ing a new identity, just as it had aimed to create *esprit de corps* at the civics. At Keele in the 1960s students were forbidden from entering the library without their gowns, which were sold alongside the more popular scarves (in Keele colours of 'tomato, egg and black pudding'),[71] whilst at the UEA bold departures from the norm of academical costume were chosen to mark the foundation of a new university for the sixties. Change was coming, however, and '... the notion that the university should separate itself off from the community, marking the distinction between students and non-students with special clothes', was beginning to be perceived as a negative one.[72] Creating a corporate identity was important for these universities but equally it was criticized from within, and the expansion of the universities opened them up to a new generation of students with whom such regulations did not sit well. Many of these gowns appeared more in regulations than on students themselves. In this period Oxbridge removed the require-ments for gown-wearing students. It has been considered that there was something of a drive from Oxbridge academics teaching at the new institutions toward the prolifer-ation of academic dress amongst staff and students on a day-to-day basis. By the end of the decade—as lecturers moved on and the culture of the new universities changed with the 'opportunity for expression captured in the zeitgeist of the 1960s'—had been eroded[73] and the later plate-glass universities did not adopt any undergraduate dress.

'Gated, gowned, and single-sex': gowns in halls of residence

Outside the well-known present-day pockets of gown-wearing amongst undergrad-uates (Oxford, Cambridge, Durham, and St Andrews), there is a number of halls of residence within the civic universities where the practice of wearing gowns at formal occasions has not entirely died out. Halls of residence were founded at these univer-sities in the late nineteenth and early twentieth century upon collegiate lines, with di-rect inspiration from life at Oxbridge colleges,[74] and have been considered the most significant development of the civic universities.[75] The first of these in England was a Church of England hall at Manchester founded in 1870, called Hulme Hall since 1887 and still open today,[76] which was followed by halls of residence across the country. It was the non-residential nature of the new universities that ensured that the undergrad-uate gowns never truly caught on, and could never really have been enforced in the first place. But in more rule-bound halls of residence gowns managed to cling on—as barely visible microcosms of Keenan's 'pockets of resistance, in which there is a gap between the university's regulations and the students' practice'.[77] At the University of Reading, Wantage Hall was built in the neo-Tudor style, complete with an impressive dining hall,

71 Keele University, *Keele's Colours and Badges*, at <www.keele.ac.uk/thekeeleoralhisto-ryproject/keeleheraldrycoloursandscarves> [retrieved 6 February 2024].

72 Whyte (2015), p. 242.

73 Sandra Wearden, 'How Academic Dress Is Mobilized in Degree Ceremonies and to What Effect', *TBS*, 15 (2015), pp. 14–29 (pp. 19–22), doi.org/10.4148/2475-7799.1131.

74 See for an example of such a foundation the original Hulme Hall Prospectus (1870), held at the University of Manchester Archive and Special Collections: GB 133 HHH/1/2.

75 Whyte (2015), p. 157.

76 J. N. Hartshorne, 'The Halls of Manchester', in University of Manchester, *Communi-cation* (Manchester: University of Manchester Communications Office, 1975), p. 12.

77 Keenan, p. 106.

in 1908.[78] A 2006 discussion on *The Student Room* (an online forum) suggests that gowns had largely fallen out of use by the late 1990s, and were worn only at significant anniversary dinners or on the high table.[79] Gowns at Wantage may since have faded from existence. The general pattern of gown-wearing at the civic universities is that it continued past requirement in lectures in an increasingly dwindling number of halls of residence, worn at an increasingly dwindling number of formal events. Whyte notes that over the 1990s 'the gated, gowned, and single-sex halls of the past were almost completely abandoned … The new residences—and the reformed versions of the old halls—were self-catering, informal, and unisex.'[80] Alongside this an orthodoxy of student opinion has grown that 'one only [lives] in hall … for just one year.'[81] This model is an economically convenient one for expanding universities, but not a positive one for the use of academic dress. There remain a few halls of residence in Britain where undergraduates wear gowns to dinner or chapel. Those presented here may not represent the entirety of current practice, as this is an area where the actual use of academic dress differs quite significantly from university regulations and as such makes research difficult; however, they likely illustrate the breadth of current usage.

Under the University of Bristol calendar of 1962—and still by the letter of the present-day regulations—Bristol undergraduates are required to wear a gown in lectures (but not labs) and 'In Halls of Residence, as required by the regulations of the Hall.'[82] In common with most universities, undergraduate gowns on the whole 'are not to be seen in the University today'.[83] There remains a small niche of gown-wearing at Bristol, however. Wills Hall was established in 1929 along the collegiate ideals already well-established as the model for a hall of residence at a civic university: one approaches up a private leafy drive, past a chapel, to a mock-gothic extravagance of sandstone and enters a quad which would not look out of place in either of England's ancient universities via a secluded porter's lodge. The practice of nightly formal hall was established by the first warden and the 'tradition of formal dining continues to this day … taken together in academic gowns.'[84] As patterns of residence (and of student expectations) changed in the 1990s Whyte describes Wills as one of the halls that remained one of the 'gated, gowned, and single-sex halls of the past',[85] though the Hall is now mixed. In 2017 it was reported in *The Tab* that all catered halls at Bristol have formal dinners; however, that at Wills they took place more frequently ('once every couple of weeks'), and that 'yes we wear gowns (not helping our case I guess).' The case in question was the hall's 'upsetting' reputation: 'known as "posh", "fancy", "for rich peo-

---

78 The layout of the Hall, and its dining hall, can be seen in Smith and Bott, p. 34. See also Holt, p. 6.

79 Holt, p. 6; <www.thestudentroom.co.uk/showthread.php?t=51614> [retrieved 7 February 2024].

80 Whyte (2015), pp. 315–16.

81 Arthur Mawby and Gerard McKenna, 'Residences and Lodgings', in Pullan, pp 142–49 (p. 148).

82 Hayward, p. 199.

83 Hayward, p. 185.

84 M. J. Crossley Evans, *A History of Wills Hall, University of Bristol*, 2nd edn (Bristol: Wills Hall Association, 2017), p. 24.

85 Whyte (2015), p. 315.

ple" amongst other, less pleasant things'.[86] It seems that the tradition of gown-wearing remains strong at Wills and enrobed undergraduates can be seen in pictures of Wills Hall as recently as 2022[87]—the 'spectacle of nearly 200 loud students in black tie and gowns' continues.[88]

Wills is rightly one of the more notable collegiate halls of residence—certainly architecturally it is perhaps the closest imitator of the ancient universities—however, it is by no means the oldest. It was at pioneering Manchester that the University's decision not to provide accommodation was first met by the establishment of halls (not at Reading, as has been claimed)[89], the first being the Anglican Hulme Hall in 1870. It was followed by Dalton Hall in 1876, a foundation of the Society of Friends; Ashburne Hall in 1901, the first women's hall; and St Anselm Hall in 1907, another Church of England venture that went on to be described as 'the closest attempt' to emulate the Oxbridge lifestyle—though its 'exclusive Anglicanism, relative poverty, and lack of influence within the university [prevented it] from doing any such thing.'[90]

The reaction to the University's introduction of undergraduate gowns at these halls was mixed. W. H. Perkins, resident of Hulme Hall in 1902, provides an interesting description of their reception, recalling that 'Hulme Hall wouldn't normally have welcomed them, but they were helpful in covering irreverent deficiencies of dress on entering chapel.' He does not say why the Hall might not have welcomed gowns.[91] The only other possible source on the reception of undergraduate cap and gown at Manchester is a debatable one, however the Lent 1902 edition of *Yggdrasill*, the magazine of Ashburne Hall, features two cherubs as its frontispiece, one wearing a cap and the other trying on a gown.[92] In any case the warden of Ashburne Hall was against the introduction of gowns in the first place, and Dalton Hall would never adopt them due to its Quaker foundation. Eventually they were brought in at Ashburne: a former resident recalled in conversation that the Junior Common Room voted to abolish them around 1990. At that point they were certainly required at Allen Hall, Hulme Hall, and St Anselm Hall most evenings, and possibly were in use at a few other halls.

At Hulme during the late 1990s gowns were unpopular owing to the expense. The JCR's solution was to purchase a set of its own gowns from Ede & Ravenscroft[93]—not Wippell & Co., as previously—which are [u3] with red cording around the yoke (a design which likely comes from the 1930s).[94] This has been the method by which undergraduate gowns are used at Hulme Hall ever since. Lowe notes that in 2002 a 'recent innovation' was a separate gown for the President of the JCR (an Oxford advanced student's

86 Ben Bloch, 'In Defence of Wills Hall', *The Bristol Tab*, 2017, at <thetab.com/uk/bristol/2017/01/08/defence-wills-hall-27879> [retrieved 7 February 2024].

87 Charles Gunter, *Wills Hall Association Yearbook 2022* (Wills Hall Association). Available at <www.willshallassociation.org/post/2022-yearbook> [retrieved 7 February 2024].

88 Crossley Evans, p. 98.

89 Holt, p. 57.

90 Whyte (2015), p. 197.

91 W. H. Perkins, quoted in the *Hulme Hall Chronicle*, 1980–81 edition, held at the University of Manchester Library Archives and Special Collections. Reference: GB 133 HHH/2/9/1.

92 Ashburne House Students, *Yggdrasill*, Lent 1902, held at the John Rylands Institute in the Ashburne Hall Archive.

93 Recounted to the author by a former resident. Also mentioned in Lowe (2002), p. 51.

94 Lowe (2002), p. 50.

gown 'with a 1" red border around the flap collar'). The whereabouts of this gown today is unknown. To offer a personal experience, when I came up to university in 2022 I had been reliably informed by recent material online that as a resident of Hulme Hall I would be issued with a gown. Gowns did not, however, appear until the second formal of the year when two former members of the JCR committee conjured up enough for the students on the high table.[95] In early 2023 we counted the JCR's gown stock (about enough for half the Hall), which had been briefly misplaced. By the February formal they were in use again. Today gowns are optional—but largely popular—for formal dinners at the Hall. There are fewer formal dinners a year at Hulme Hall today than in the past, and the freshers' handbook for the 2023–24 academic year at Hulme Hall has toned down its terms from 'Wearing gowns to formal meals is a requirement for residency'[96] (in 2003) to: '... undergraduate gowns ... will be offered by the JCR free of charge ... Postgraduates are welcome to wear any other academic dress to which they are entitled.'[97]

St Anselm Hall likely adopted gowns around 1922 'following the pattern of Hulme'[98] and today they are required for frequent formal dinners and at weekly chapel—the Hall is considered something of an incongruity in Manchester for these traditions.[99] From 2021 to 2023 there were protests at St Anselm Hall against wearing gowns to three dinners a week, which led to dinner boycotts and eventually a table for students not wearing gowns was permitted. Despite this gowns remain fairly popular at the Hall and the more relaxed nature of regular formals (compared to less frequent dinners at Hulme or Wills, where most students wear formal attire under their gowns) has led to the adoption of something like the St Andrews' approach to undergraduate gowns: thrown quickly over casual clothing.[100] Although the attitude can hardly be described as going beyond events where gowns are required, the Hall has worn gowns for such impromptu ceremonials as the 'funeral of "Eric" the hedgehog' in 2019.[101] Since the recent closure of the Hall bar, gangs of undergraduates in gowns walking across Victoria Park in search of refreshment are not an unknown sight.

Manchester and Bristol seem to be the main pockets of gown-wearing. The only other example I have been able to find of recent years is that of Devonshire Hall at the University of Leeds, which opened in 1928. It was structured in the 'traditional "Oxbridge" style'[102] and there is some evidence that gowns are still in use for formal dinners. The Hall information page on the University's website included a quote from a student that 'Our formal dinners are great; everyone dresses up and wears University

95   It should be noted that as Manchester halls do not have fellows or academic staff, the high table is used by the pastoral staff, the executive committee of the JCR, and any guests.

96   Hulme Hall, *Residents' Handbook*, 2002–03, held at the University of Manchester Library Archive and Special Collections. Reference: GB 133 HHH/2/10/14.

97   Hulme Hall JCR, *Welcome Hulme, Information* (pamphlet in small circulation).

98   Lowe (2002), p. 52.

99   Ella Robinson, 'Slems Is Known As the Weirdest University Halls in Manchester. That's Exactly How the Students Like it', *The Mill*, 25 November 2023, at <manchestermill .co.uk/p/slems-is-known-as-the-weirdest-university> [retrieved 28 April 2024].

100   Keenan, pp. 105–06.

101   St Anselm Hall Association, 'Life in Hall', *St Anselm Hall Archive*, at <stanselmhall .wixsite.com/stanselmhallarchive/blank>.

102   University of Leeds Conferences and Events, *Devonshire Hall*, at <conferencesand events.leeds.ac.uk/devonshire-hall/> [retrieved 7 February 2024].

Fig. 15. A formal dinner at St. Anselm Hall in October 2020.

Fig. 16. Students in Manchester undergraduate gowns in the Hulme Hall bar before a formal dinner, February 2023.

robes to have a sit-down meal together'[103] though the current page does not mention academic dress.[104] Groves has suggested that a 'mystery item' shown to members of the Burgon Society—'an aged undergraduate gown with bell sleeves and facings edged with pinkish/red ribbon and red corded yoke' – could have come from a Leeds hall,[105] though this description seems to fit the Victoria University of Manchester students' gown held in the Burgon Society Archives (Fig. 3).[106]

Were it not for the halls it is conceivable that Manchester undergraduate dress could never have progressed beyond a mention at the 1902 jubilee, and that with the removal of enforced requirements to wear gowns in lectures at Bristol they too would have vanished; however, these institutions must be credited almost entirely with keeping the tradition of undergraduate dress not only nominally present but a living part of day-to-day student life in small parts of a few civic universities. Though these universities as a whole are not necessarily those 'at which "tradition" is embraced' to an institutional degree, these halls should be considered a part of the 'growing pockets of resistance', noted by Keenan.[107] This gap is clear. Even as undergraduate dress slipped out of university calendars it remained a part of hall regulations at a number of traditional halls, and though it has fallen out of use steadily alongside the decline of formal dinners it remains a part of hall life in the twenty-first century.

Other uses of undergraduate dress

In most universities the day-to-day wearing of academic dress has all-but vanished. Beyond halls of residence it should be noted that some universities have found re-

---

103   University of Leeds. Devonshire Hall, at <web.archive.org/web/20210419060328 /https:/accommodation.leeds.ac.uk/residence/4/devonshire-hall> [retrieved 7 February 2024).

104   University of Leeds. *Devonshire Hall*, at <accommodation.leeds.ac.uk/residence/4 /devonshire-hall> [retrieved 7 February 2024].

105   Philip Lowe, 'And a Good Time Was Had by All ... in Manchester', *Burgon Notes*, 20 (June 2012), pp. 2–3 (p. 3), at <burgon.org.uk/about-us/notes>.

106   See images WBS-284 (f) and WBS-284 (b) <burgon.org.uk/archive/victoria -manchester> [retrieved 28 April 2024].

107   Keenan, p. 106.

formed use for their undergraduate gowns and that others have seen a surprising length of use: At St David's College Lampeter the undergraduate gowns—of which there were variations for scholars[108]—remained in use until 1971. Today student petitions to reinstate gown-wearing at modern universities would be surprising to say the least, certainly if they were followed by significant support. The unique undergraduate gown of the UEA was not mentioned in a 2015 suggestion from the international student ambassadors that formal dinners be brought in at the university.[109]

At several universities the undergraduate gown has morphed into an usher's gown to be worn at ceremonies—this could stem from practice employed at least at Manchester whereby undergraduates were paid to be ushers but were required to wear an undergraduate gown, long after the gowns' official status had vanished. It should be noted that Manchester since seems to have adopted a purple gown with a yellow stripe around the yoke for the use of ushers at ceremonies—bearing a similar design to the old undergraduate gowns, but also to previously used stewards' gowns.[110]

> [A]nyone attending a graduation ceremony of the University [of Bradford] would see a great number of individuals wearing undergraduate gowns … usually undergraduates assisting with the ceremony or other individuals who are not entitled to wear any other form of academic dress.[111]

Jackson reveals that Manchester undergraduate gowns have 'been pressed into service on a largely ad hoc basis as ushers' gowns at a number of other British universities' including Warwick,[112] which never specified any undergraduate dress.[113] It is of note that whilst this could be considered the adoption of robes for officers, other universities specify bachelors' gowns for non-graduates participating in ceremonies.[114] Even at universities where academic dress is rarely seen, the occasion of a graduation remains a spectacle of hoods and gowns where universities show themselves in their full quasi-medieval splendour. Similar occasions have resurrected the undergraduate gown at Manchester, with 'unexpected' use of the undergraduate gown at royal visits as late as 1959.[115]

Student officials have also been enrobed. At the University of Exeter between the years 1962 and 1997 the scholars' gown was 'worn exclusively by the president of the Students' Guild on very formal occasions, such as attendance at the University Court',[116] and at Bradford a set of unique gowns was designed for the officers of the Stu-

---

108 Shaw (2011), p. 238.

109 Chau Nguye, 'Hall Dinner in UEA Why Not?', *UEA Notes from Norfolk* (2015) <uea-notesfromnorfolk.blogspot.com/2015/08/hall-dinner-in-uea-why-not.html> [retrieved 22 June 2024].

110 Lowe (2002), p. 49.

111 Clarke, pp. 25–26.

112 Nicholas Jackson, 'The Development of Academic Dress in the University of Warwick', *TBS*, 8 (2008), pp. 19–58 (p. 34), doi.org/10.4148/2475-7799.1061.

113 Shaw (2011), p. 416.

114 An example of this is the University of Stirling. See Colin Fleming, 'The Academical Dress of the University of Stirling, 1967–2006', *TBS*, 6 (2006), pp. 54–76 (p. 60), doi.org/10.4148/2475-7799.1050.

115 Lowe (2002), p. 49.

116 Quy, p. 44.

dents' Union: 'not strictly undergraduate gowns in the traditional sense, they certainly constitute part of the academic dress for some undergraduates.'[117] On occasion the odd tradition has kept undergraduate dress in use, though not as generally as in the halls.

Conclusions

The vast majority of the UK's universities have been established since 1880, and there has been an evident decline in the adoption of undergraduate academical dress as time has gone on and the level of formality associated with university life has decreased. Most of the universities established between 1880 and 1960 either have or have had some form of undergraduate academic dress; however, only one post-1992 university has done the same.

Academic dress, at both the civic and plate-glass universities, was conceived as a means to create a single body corporate amongst the staff and students of the university; however, the differing approaches to university life at the largely non-residential civics in comparison to Oxbridge did not permit the widespread use of undergraduate costume to continue for a great length of time, as it has at the ancient universities. Halls of residence at the civics aimed to bring something of college life into the new universities and succeeded in ensuring the survival of academic dress to the present-day in a few cases. A few plate-glass universities experimented with enforcing academical dress upon their undergraduate students; however, this was not successful in the face of changing university culture during the 1960s, and it seems that by 1970 none of the then-new universities even encouraged the wearing of gowns in lectures.

In 1909 the University of Bristol gowns committee discovered that gowns were regularly worn by undergraduates at Cambridge, Oxford, Durham, Newcastle, Bangor, Cardiff, and St Andrews (and further research should have added Lampeter and Aberystwyth to that list); worn occasionally at Glasgow and Aberdeen; and used for ceremony at London, Manchester, and Birmingham. Today it seems that academical dress is regularly worn by undergraduates at Cambridge, Oxford, Durham, and St Andrews; worn occasionally at Manchester, Bristol, and possibly at Leeds and Reading; and used by ushers at Bradford, Warwick, and possibly at other institutions.

Acknowledgements

Chris Williams took the photos in the Burgon Society Archive. Figure 1 is reproduced with the kind permission of Nick Chadwick. Figure 2 is reproduced with the kind permission of Alex Kerr. Figures 7 and 8 are reproduced with the kind permission of John Horton.

---

117   Clarke, p. 26.

Transactions of the Burgon Society, 23 (2023), pages 94–109

The Contemporary Usage of Academic Hoods in Oxford Collegiate Choirs

By Samuel Teague

The question of hood-wearing etiquette within choirs has always been something of a contentious one. Many who have followed this line of inquiry will know the work of the late Dr Nicholas Groves,[1] whose article explored many of the myths surrounding hood-wearing in a choir environment. However, despite this, arguments still persist— and, regardless of what the Canons say (be they the 1604 or 1969 revisions), tradition and personal opinion still seem to win out in most cases.

For evidence for the use of hoods, a primary source is the *Book of Common Prayer*, first issued in 1549 under Edward VI, which requires inclusion of hoods as part of the dress code for a number of institutions, including college chapels.

Further reference to the wearing of such items in the Ornaments Rubric is to be found in the 1559 Act of Uniformity and reissue of the *Book of Common Prayer* (following Elizabeth I's accession).[2]

> Provided always, and be it enacted, that such ornaments of the church, and of the ministers thereof, shall be retained and be in use, as was in the Church of England, by authority of Parliament, in the second year of the reign of King Edward VI, until other order shall be therein taken by the authority of the queen's majesty, with the advice of her commissioners appointed and authorized, under the great seal of England, for causes ecclesiastical, or of the metropolitan of this realm.[3]

> ... that the Minister at the time of the Communion, and at all other times in his Ministration, and all use such Ornaments in the Church, as were in use by authority of Parliament in the second yeere of the Reigne of Edward the sixt according to the Acte of Parliament set foorth in the beginning of thys Booke.[4]

The meaning here is, famously, disputed but can be read in support of the wearing of such vestments and ornaments as laid down in the 1549 *Book of Common Prayer*.[5]

---

1 Nicholas Groves, 'The Use of the Academic Hood in Quire', *TBS*, 8 (2008), pp. 98–105.
2 This is the common term by which this passage is known. See, 'Ornaments Rubric.' *The Concise Oxford Dictionary of the Christian Church* (Oxford University Press, 2014) at Oxford Reference <www-oxfordreference-com.ezproxy-prd.bodleian.ox.ac.uk/display/10.1093/acref/9780199659623.001.0001/acref-9780199659623-e-4229?rskey=vgQH87&result=4301> [retrieved 23 June 2024 but requires permission to access]. The term 'ornament' when referring to hoods was preferred by the Revd Percy Dearmer, as the term 'robes' is too general, and 'vestments' too specific to the garments worn for the Eucharist. See Dearmer, *The Ornaments of the Ministers* (London: A. R. Mowbray, 1920), p. 3.
3 Act of Uniformity, 1559.
4 *Book of Common Prayer*, 1559.
5 For recent contributions on and around the debate concerning the Ornaments Ru-

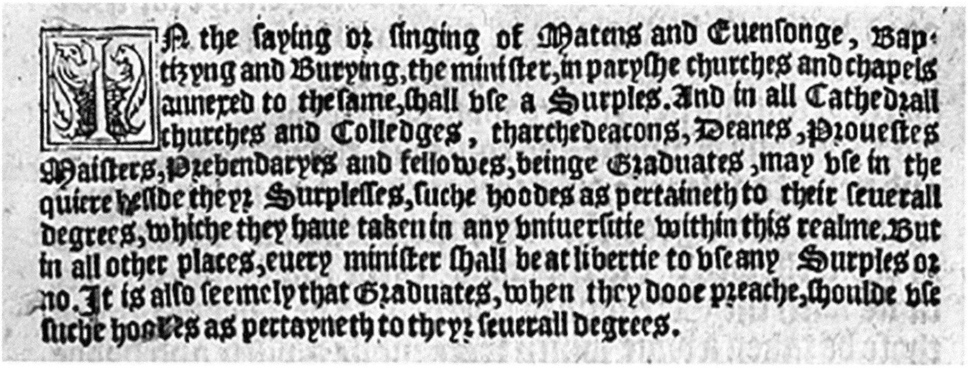

In the saying or singing of Matens and Euensonge, Baptzyng and Burying, the minister, in parysshe churches and chapels annexed to the same, shall use a Surples. And in all Cathedrall churches and Colledges, tharchedeacons, Deanes, Prouestes Maisters, Prebendaryes and fellowes, beinge Graduates, may use in the quiere beside theyr Surplesses, suche hoodes as pertaineth to their seuerall degrees, whiche they haue taken in any vniuersitie within this realme. But in all other places, euery minister shall be at libertie to vse any Surples or no. It is also seemely that Graduates, when they dooe preache, shoulde vse suche hoodes as pertayneth to theyr seuerall degrees.

Fig. 1. Instructions from the 1549 Book of Common Prayer, at f.157v, detailing the usage of hoods within services.

This is the interpretation used by the Revd Percy Dearmer and, for the sake of this article, will be the stance adopted by this author also. Thus, the wearing of academic hoods in collegiate chapels can be traced to amongst the earliest roots of worship in the Church of England.

Of course, the rubric, as printed in the 1549 *Book of Common Prayer*, avoids explicit reference to musicians,[6] but one should consider the development of choir personnel in such a collegiate institution. Choir membership (for those who may be entitled to wear hoods) has steadily evolved from consisting solely of clergy, through the introduction of lay clerks, and finally to the introduction of choral scholarships and, just as notably, the admission of women. Therefore, the rubrics laid down in 1549 and 1559 can be seen to apply to collegiate choirs today, remaining applicable even with the evolution of personnel.

The relevant Canons mentioned by Groves in his article are reproduced below, cited from *The Book of Church Law*. The first, Canon 17 of 1604, details the usage of dress in the chapels of collegiate institutions:

> All masters and fellows of colleges or halls, and all the scholars and students in either of the universities, shall, in their churches and chapels, upon all Sundays, holydays, and their eves, at the time of Divine Service, wear surplices, according to the order of the Church of England: and such as are graduates shall agreeably wear with their surplices such hoods as do severally appertain unto their degrees.[7]

And secondly, Canon 25 stipulates the following:

---

bric, see Dan D. Cruickshank, 'Debating the Legal Status of the Ornaments Rubric: Ritualism and Royal Commissions in Late Nineteenth- and Early Twentieth-Century England', *Studies in Church History*, 56 (2020), pp. 434–54; and Bryan D. Spinks, 'The Intersection of "English Use" Liturgy and Social Justice: Snapshots of Augustus Pugin, Percy Dearmer, Conrad Noel and William Palmer Ladd', *Journal of Anglican Studies*, 19 (2021), pp. 21–36.

6   An intention of reformers being to indicate a licence (and authority) to preach through the conferral of the MA and the wearing of the hood—degrees being presented *ad incipiendum in eadem facultate* (to incept in the same faculty).

7   J. H. Blunt, rev. W. G. F. Phillimore and G. E. Jones, *The Book of Church Law*, 10th edn (London: Longmans, Green, 1905), p. 378.

> When there is no Communion it shall suffice to wear surplices; saving that all deans, masters, and heads of collegiate churches, canons, and prebendaries, being graduates, shall daily, at the time of prayer and preaching wear with their surplices such hoods as are agreeable to their degrees.[8]

The most recent printed edition of *The Canons of the Church of England* (Section B8) makes no mention of the wearing of hoods as an ornament for the clergy, let alone for those in the choir.[9] Interestingly, however, there is mention in the Royal School of Church Music's *The Voice for Life Chorister's Companion* which states that: 'At some services (usually Morning or Evening Prayer) an academic hood may be worn by the minister or by members of the choir. Hoods mark the award of a university degree or diploma.'[10] Although this statement does little to offer any explanation (understandable, given the target audience), it does give some foundation to the wearing of hoods in any choir setting, and not necessarily just collegiate.

This article presents my research into the usage of academic hoods in Oxford collegiate choirs today. It aims to provide a record of the current situation, whilst not re-treading ground covered in Groves's article. The history of, and rules for wearing academic dress at Oxford will be explored, before moving on to view the data collected from choir members and their directors. This will be used to assess the state of the practice in the collegiate choirs at Oxford, and an overview of contemporary usage. It should be assumed that most of the discussion which follows centres on practice for Evensong, which represents the overwhelming majority of their engagements.

Methodology

To provide a thorough basis for this inquiry, a two-stage approach was adopted. The first stage sought to engage the Organists/Directors of Music[11] in order to ascertain their views and approaches towards the wearing of academic dress (namely, hoods) in the setting of the collegiate choirs of which they were in charge. The aim was to provide a strong and objective baseline of information, from which some preliminary conclusions might be drawn. In order to focus this inquiry, it was decided that only the sixteen collegiate choirs that participate in the choral and organ awards (and therefore operate under the leadership of an appointed director) would be assessed. The information collected, and conclusions reached as a result, are correct as of the end of Trinity Term 2023 (mid-June).

The second stage was to approach current members of Oxford collegiate choirs, via questionnaire, to gauge the understanding of and attitudes towards the wearing of academic dress in the choir(s) of which they were members. The responses from this second stage could then be compared to the responses and baseline provided by the

---

8   Ibid., p. 381.

9   Church of England, *The Canons of the Church of England 2022*, 8th edn (London: Church House, 2022), p. 25.

10   Tim Ruffer, *The Voice for Life Chorister's Companion* (Salisbury: RSCM, 2009), p. 132.

11   Historically, the title of the individual in charge of the choir has been given as 'Organist', despite the fact that the directing of the choir might well preclude the playing of said instrument. Increasingly, the title 'Director of Music' is used, which removes the confusion and (often) stipulation that the director may be expected to play the organ.

first, allowing an overall assessment of the contemporary usage of academic hoods in the collegiate choirs of Oxford.

I have been a lay clerk with the Choir of The Queen's College for four years (on top of an initial year as a graduate scholar). My position on the matter is that those entitled to do so should wear their hoods when appropriate. This now aligns with common usage in the choir at the end of the 2022–23 academic year, but was not the case upon joining (in 2019) and goes to illustrate potential change in attitudes and practice over a small period.

Academic dress in Oxford

The wearing of academic dress for events in colleges varies widely. Some require one to wear a gown at formal hall (with few stipulations for the rest of one's chosen outfit; certainly not requiring subfusc), whereas others require such infrequent wearing that students may get rid of their gowns after the matriculation ceremony, only then to have to buy them again for examinations.

In 2015, a referendum was held by the Oxford University Student Union in which members were asked if they would support the continued wearing of subfusc for examinations. This resulted in 75.8 per cent of voters opting to keep subfusc, and 24.2 per cent voting to get rid of it.[12] An additional vote saw a similar question asked concerning the compulsory wearing of a gown and cap: the vote was similarly in favour of upholding the tradition, at 78 per cent to 22 per cent. Whilst both motions did not result in resolutions to dilute the wearing of academic dress, they both reflect the sentiment of a not insignificant (and ever-growing) faction in Oxford who believe that academic dress is archaic and off-putting to those from non-privately educated backgrounds.[13]

But these discussions apply only to gowns and subfusc; the wearing of hoods is even less common, and the guidance for what is required for University-level events beyond that of matriculation and examinations can be somewhat difficult to decipher. The University of Oxford does have established levels of academic dress, which can be found in three recent sources: John Venables' 2009 book, *Academic Dress of the University of Oxford*;[14] the Vice-Chancellor's Regulations 1 (2002, rev. 2008, 2012,

---

12 Damien Gayle, 'Oxford University Students Vote to Keep "Archaic" Subfusc Academic Dress', *Guardian*, 23 May 2015.

13 It should also be noted that, even if the referendum had resulted in a resolution to make the wearing of subfusc or gowns/caps non-compulsory, the Student Union does not have the authority to change the regulations of the University—rather it would have then lobbied for change which the University would have been able to reject outright.

Additionally, one might also consider participation bias when assessing the results of the referendum. The proportion of members of the University of Oxford who actively vote in Student Union matters is low; this is because the colleges and their respective common rooms fulfil many of the same roles that a students' union would in a non-collegiate university. With this in mind, it is probable that a poll of the entire University body would produce a different result, perhaps more emphatically in favour of maintaining academic dress.

14 (Oxford: Shepherd & Woodward, 2009) p. 49. On the development of academic dress at the University of Oxford, see Andrew James Peter North, 'The Development of the Academic Dress of the University of Oxford 1920–2012', *TBS*, 13 (2013), pp. 101–41.

2015);[15] and the most recent Academic Dress Guidance Table (2024).[16] The first two sources split the dress code between 'Bachelors and Masters', and 'Doctors', as follows:

Bachelors and Masters
1. Black gown
2. Black gown and hood
3. Black gown, hood, square (or for women, a soft cap if preferred), and *subfusc* (full academic dress)
4. Black gown, hood, square (or for women, a soft cap if preferred) *subfusc*, and bands

Doctors
5. Black (laced except for DD)
6. Black gown and hood
7. Black gown, hood, square (or for women, a soft cap if preferred), and *subfusc*
8. Convocation habit (black gown, hood, and sleeveless cloak (chimere), square (or for women, a soft cap if preferred), *subfusc*, and bands)
9. Scarlet robe and appropriate cap
10. Scarlet robe with *subfusc* (full academic dress for DPhils)
11. Scarlet robe with *subfusc*, bands, and the appropriate cap (full academic dress for higher doctorates)

This is streamlined in the most recent official guidance from the University, collating the separate 'Bachelors and Masters' and 'Doctors' segments into one, resulting in just seven levels of dress:[17]

1. Black gown (For Doctors except DD: laced)
2. Black gown and hood
3. Black gown, hood, cap (square or soft permitted) and subfusc
4. Black gown, hood, cap, *subfusc* and bands or Convocation habit for Doctors (chemir worn over the black undress gown and hood, *subfusc*, cap and bands)
5. Scarlet robe and appropriate cap
6. Scarlet robe, cap and *subfusc* (Full Academic Dress for DPhils)
7. Scarlet robe with *subfusc* and bands and appropriate cap (Full Academic Dress for Higher Doctors)

All three sources then go on to specify the level of dress required for each event. It is clear from formatting alone that the Guidance Table is an updated form of Venables' work, with both providing three columns indicating the required level of dress for bachelors and masters, DPhils, and higher doctors. When the two tables are compared it is interesting to observe that in the singular instance levels of dress are not the same, there is a lowering of the level of dress required. 'General' Church services previously required DPhils and higher doctors to wear their hoods (and Convocation habits, if desired),[18] but the most recent guidance has lowered this to gowns only. The Court Sermon procession is now the only occasion where a higher level of required dress has been maintained from earlier versions of guidance (levels 2 or 4 on the Guid-

---

15 University of Oxford. Vice-Chancellor's Regulations 1 of 2002. Amended 24 January 2008, 19 July 2012 and 7 August 2015 (*Gazette*, Vol. 145 (23 July 2015), pp. 694–96), <governance .admin.ox.ac.uk/legislation/vice-chancellors-regulations-1-of-2002> [retrieved 29 May 2024].

16 Academic Dress Guidance Table at <www.ox.ac.uk/sites/files/oxford/Dress_Code _Guideline_table.pdf> [retrieved 29 May 2024].

17 Ibid.

18 'General' is the term that the sources use to refer to normal church services.

Table 1. University events when the wearing of a hood is specified.
Where two readings are given, this represents a differentiation between bachelors and masters, and doctors.

Event	Venables (2009)	VC Regulations (2002–15)	Guidance Table (2024)
Chancellor's court of benefactors	Y	Y	Y
Church services (general, funerals/memorials, weekdays)	N/Y	N/Y	N
Church services (court sermon)	N/Y	N/Y	N/Y
Gazette days	Y	Y	Y
Orations and admissions	Y	Y	Y
Degree ceremonies	Y	Y	Y
Encaenia and royal visits	Y	Y	Y
Examinations	Y	Y	Y
Garden parties	Y	Y	—
Delivering a major public lecture	Y	Y	Y
Admission of proctors and pro-proctors	Y	Y	Y
Admission of Vice-Chancellor, Pro-Vice-Chancellors, and clerks of the market	Y	Y	Y

ance Table, and then only for DPhils and higher doctors). Thus, as we consider the events where one might be required to wear a hood, we must do so in an environment where occasions for wearing academic dress are already small in number, appear to be gradually increasing in their scarcity, and are often confusing depending on which of the three sources one chooses to consult.[19] The events at which the wearing of a hood is specified (in at least one of the three sources) can be seen in Table 1, above.

Whilst the guidance largely agrees on those events when one would be required wear a hood, what should be stressed is the infrequency with which they occur in any given year and, crucially in regard to this article, how they might coincide with choir events. The most obvious crossovers are church services, but the most up-to-date guidance suggests that one should wear a hood only at Court Sermons (and even then, only if one is part of the procession). Conspicuous in its absence is any mention of University Sermons in any of the three sources. The University Sermon is perhaps the most common University event to intersect with the activities of collegiate choirs in Oxford, as the sermons rotate through the chapels (and University Church) in a predetermined pattern.[20] Therefore, it is strange (if perhaps an oversight) that there is no prescribed guidance on academic dress for these services.

---

19 For the sake of this article, it is assumed that the Academic Dress Guidance Table is the authoritative document, having been issued directly from the University, and as the most up-to-date document.

20 For a list of recent University Sermons and their locations in the collegiate University see University Church. University Sermons, at <www.universitychurch.ox.ac.uk/content/university -sermons> [retrieved 30 May 2024].

Additionally, it is not uncommon for one of the college choirs to be asked to perform at some of the other events listed in Table 1, such as Encaenia (where one college choir performs each year, on a loose rota), but as the events are not chapel services, concert dress or cassocks (without surplices and, therefore, also without hoods), are usually adopted.

What should also be noted is that the above rules apply specifically to academic dress of the University, and do not apply to any hoods granted by a degree from another institution—therefore a graduate in the University possessing a Bachelor of Arts degree from another institution would not be allowed to wear their hood with Oxford academic dress, instead having to opt for their black gown (and subfusc, where appropriate) alone. These rules, however, do not (usually) apply for a regular chapel service if hoods are permitted for those in the choir. This being said, the Vice-Chancellor's Regulations of 2002 allow for the wearing of non-Oxford academic dress (to which one is entitled) at any event where they 'would otherwise be required to wear the academic dress of the University', with the exception of degree ceremonies and Encaenia.[21] Therefore, it is wearing the hood of another institution on top of Oxford academic dress alone that is incompatible with the regulations of the University.

Academic hoods and Oxford collegiate choirs

For something so seemingly innocuous, the wearing of academic hoods within choirs can cause great rifts within collegiate environments. These rifts often become pronounced when there is a change in practice, especially at the point of the introduction of a culture of hood-wearing, which can generate a great deal of animosity.[22]

One would expect the tradition of hood-wearing to be strongest within the collegiate chapel, after all, those in the immediate environs are people who often own their own academic dress. Whilst this may have been true well into the twentieth century, these traditions are not as actively upheld, nor appreciated.[23]

Regarding the nature of the collegiate choir itself, the choral and organ awards see prospective undergraduates apply for their scholarships over a year before their entry into the University. This results in the sixteen collegiate choirs which admit by the awards scheme being heavily dominated by undergraduates, with positions for graduates and professional clerks being sparse (but gradually increasing).[24] Therefore, the result is the inevitable fact that the majority of collegiate choristers will not have a degree which entitles them to an academic hood,[25] leaving those graduates who are entitled in the minority. From this author's own experience (as well as further anec-

---

21 Vice-Chancellor's Regulations 1 of 2002, Clause 3.

22 Any animosity seems particularly focused amongst younger members of the choirs: those who are not yet entitled to wear a hood. It is an attitude that, from both personal observation and conversation, changes once they have graduated.

23 One need only compare pictures of college life (both planned and candid) from the early- to mid-twentieth century and more recently to observe the change in attitude, as is discussed in the following paragraphs.

24 The prevalence of graduate choral scholarships has, however, been increasing in the past few years. Clerkships at the foundations are more consistent, with numbers fluctuating in the other ensembles.

25 This is purposefully ignoring hoods granted by diplomas, such as the Trinity College Licentiates Hood (LTCL).

dotal evidence), the smaller number of choristers with the right to wear hoods can sometimes create an odd atmosphere within a choir, where—through confusion in the practice, frustration at the perception of someone thinking they are senior/superior, disruption of uniformity, or perhaps even envy—the practice of wearing a hood can become toxic.

However, one should not to dismiss all the perceived issues with the wearing of academic hoods out of hand, particularly concerning uniformity. These issues tie into many conversations about being presented as equals within the environment of a church, which Groves did touch upon in his article,[26] and is only exacerbated when only one or two members of the choir are graduates entitled to wear hoods—further segueing into the discussion of internal hierarchies and perceptions of seniority/superiority.

Up to this point the entitlement to wear a hood has been assumed to accompany the conferment of a degree but this is not necessarily the case. Professional qualifications entitle many musicians to wear an academic hood well before they graduate from university with a degree. The most common are the diploma qualifications, from the Associated Board of the Royal Schools of Music (DipABRSM and ARSM)[27] and Trinity College London (LTCL) which many will have achieved prior to arriving in the Oxford collegiate choir scene. Additionally, those who play the organ (particularly those who are scholars on the instrument) may have already achieved or will work towards those diplomas offered by the Royal College of Organists across the duration of their scholarships/degrees: first the Associate of the Royal College of Organists (ARCO) and then the Fellowship (FRCO), each level with a different hood.

Therefore, what may be concluded from the above is that whilst there is still a strong tradition of academic dress within the University of Oxford and its constituent colleges, occasions when hooded dress is required are infrequent; those entitled to wear hoods are often in a minority; and should a University occasion arise when the wearing of a hood is appropriate, said wearing of the hood is often incompatible within the choral setting. In addition, the practice of hood-wearing within the collegiate choirs themselves is an almost entirely separate tradition, with the potential variety of external hoods being quite pronounced, and the decision as to whether the wearing is allowed being in the hands (functionally, at least) of the Organist/Director of Music or Chaplain.[28]

At least in the case of The Queen's College, true authority in deciding conventions on wearing academic dress (and by extension, hoods) during services lies with the Governing Body. However, this is not a question which has ever been raised, and unless such a conversation should occur, functional decisions regarding dress reside with the Organist/Director of Music and Chaplain. Historically, members of the College, both junior and senior, would have to wear gowns when attending services in the chapel. This was never included in the statutes or bylaws, but rather official practice as mandated by the Governing Body. The tradition is now only regularly upheld by senior members and, despite having never been rescinded by the Governing Body, the wear-

---

26 Groves, p. 102.

27 DipABRSM was discontinued at the end of 2023.

28 Further work on this topic might include a survey of the Chaplain of each chapel as, in some instances, his or her view on the wearing of hoods may be as important as that of the Director of Music (if not more so).

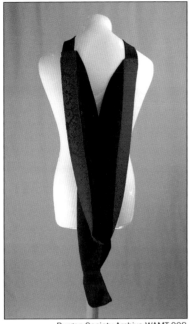

Fig. 2. Common non-degree academic hoods to which choir members may be entitled.

Fig. 2A (left): Associate of the Royal College of Organists. Fig. 2B (right): Licentiate of the Trinity College, London.

ing of gowns for services is not enforced for junior members.[29] Therefore, in addition to the intricacies of University regulations against collegiate practice, what should occur in any given chapel (i.e., gowns being worn by all members, and presumably hoods, when entitled and appropriate) is not necessarily what does occur.

Contemporary usage of academic hoods

Two separate questionnaires were circulated to those sixteen choirs which admit members through the choral and organ awards scheme,[30] one to the directors, and a second to the members of the choirs.

It should be noted that the type of collegiate choir in Oxford varies among colleges. The three choral foundations, Christ Church, Magdalen College, and New College,[31] operate in a manner more closely akin to that of a cathedral (Christ Church, of course, being the Cathedral for the See of Oxford since 1546).[32] This means one might expect an active tradition of hood-wearing; however, as will be seen below, this is not the case for these institutions. The three foundations are accompanied by a further

---

29 I am indebted to the Revd Peter Southwell (Chaplain of The Queen's College, Oxford, 1982–2010) for his accounts of practice at the College and University, as well as his input across several drafts of this article.

30 These being: Brasenose, Christ Church, Exeter, Harris Manchester, Keble, Magdalen, Merton, New, Oriel, Pembroke, Queen's, St Edmund Hall, St Peter's, Somerville, University, Worcester.

31 The provision for chorister scholarships exists within the original foundation statutes of each college, with each having an attached school from which these choristers are drawn.

32 Judith Curthoys, *The King's Cathedral: The Ancient Heart of Christ Church, Oxford* (London: Profile Books, 2019), p. 74.

three college choirs which operate with child choristers. Both Pembroke and Worcester Colleges have choristers with scholarships based in Christ Church Cathedral School, available for those boys who do not hold scholarships for the main Cathedral choir, and since 2016, Merton College has operated a girls' choir drawing choristers from local schools, and who sing on Mondays and Wednesdays.[33]

There is then a group of choirs which wear cassocks and surplices (Pembroke, Worcester, and Merton), and another group which opts to wear gowns instead. From these three, albeit rough, categories of collegiate choirs in Oxford one might extrapolate a tiered approach to the wearing of hoods within the constituent colleges of the University, consistent with the level of choir dress they adopt.

From the data collected, the dress code for those choirs which admit members via the choral and organ awards appears in Table 2.

The raw data illustrates a large variety across the collegiate choirs. Whilst there is a good amount of strong opposition to the wearing of academic hoods—reasoning for which we will examine below—there is no matching force on the other end of the spectrum; rather there is a marked ambivalence towards the practice. To paraphrase several conversations that took place during the course of the research, it would seem that most directors do not care whether their members wear hoods, as long as the music still sounds good. Additionally, whether choir members are permitted to wear hoods is not always necessarily at the discretion of the choir director. In at least two instances above, direction from the Chaplain has been the deciding factor. Suffice it to say, seniority (in regard to the internal hierarchy of the college) tends to hold sway in such decisions.

The reasoning for opposition to the wearing of hoods varies, but there seem to be three grounds for such opposition:

1. Incompatibility with base dress code (i.e., gowns)
2. Lack of uniformity/promotes elitism
3. Distraction from worship

The first of these is simple enough to understand. The addition of a hood to the wearing of one's academic gown essentially elevates the dress code to one that is reserved for some of the most significant university events (such as Encaenia and graduation ceremonies), and therefore would be inappropriate in the majority of instances.

The reasoning that the addition of hoods ruins uniformity would seem to be the most strongly held opposition to the practice, and one can understand why. With an ensemble such as a choir, a sense of unity and cohesion is an important factor, so differentiating oneself from the crowd is often perceived to have the opposite impact. This is sometimes perceived as going so far as to promote a form of elitism within the group. A further contributing factor to this argument comes as an unlikely (though, perhaps, inevitable) side-effect to Covid-19: the livestreaming of services. Since March 2020, there has been a marked increase in the introduction of livestreaming equipment in many of the Oxford college chapels. The sudden bounds in exposure to new audiences all over the world have necessitated, in some instances, a rethink in how choirs present themselves. At the end of Trinity Term 2023, for instance, the choir of

33 Merton College Girl Choristers, at <www.merton.ox.ac.uk/merton-college-girl-choristers> [retrieved 17 July 2023].

Table 2. Information on dress code and usage of hoods within the sixteen collegiate choirs which admit choristers through the choral awards scheme.

Choir	Dress Code	Director	Choristers
Brasenose	Academic gowns	Does not wear a hood	Wearing of hoods is permitted
Christ Church	Cassocks and surplices	Does not wear a hood	Not permitted to wear hoods
Exeter	Cassocks and surplices	Would wear a hood if entitled	Wearing of hoods is permitted, but is not common practice
Harris Manchester	Academic gowns	Does not wear a hood	Not permitted to wear hoods
Keble	Cassocks and surplices	Wears a hood when directing services, when deemed necessary	Wearing of hoods is permitted[1]
Magdalen	Cassocks and surplices	Will usually wear a hood when directing services	Hoods are not commonly worn and are permitted only at a small number of pre-determined special services/occasions during the year
Merton	Cassocks and surplices	Often wears a hood during Evensong	Only Oxford hoods are permitted
New	Cassocks and surplices	Does not wear a hood	Not permitted to wear hoods
Oriel	Cassocks and surplices	Elects not to wear a hood as they view the practice as an intrusion to, and distraction from, worship	Wearing of hoods is permitted, left to the conscience of each individual member
Pembroke	Robes[2]	Wears a hood when directing services	Wearing of hoods is currently not feasible over the robes (not academic gowns), but will be allowed once dress code transitions

1 Practice briefly changed during Hilary Term 2023, taking advantage of the temporary departure of the Chaplain, who enforced the hood-wearing policy. Non-Oxford graduates took the opportunity to wear their hoods without repercussion before the standard policy was reinforced.
2 To transition to cassocks and surplices for the academic year beginning Michaelmas Term 2023.

Choir	Dress Code	Director	Choristers
Queen's	Cassocks and surplices	Usually elects to not wear a hood unless essential (see, University Sermons), but increasingly will wear a hood on Sunday so to match the usage of other members	Wearing of hoods is permitted. Currently, usage is reserved for Sundays and special services, such as feast days, at the discretion of the choir members. The choir in the 2022/23 academic year had a higher than usual intake of graduates, which aided in the changing of standard practice
St Edmund Hall	Academic gowns	Wears a hood when directing services	Wearing of hoods is permitted, but is not common practice, as the addition of a hood to the gown (rather than over a cassock and surplice) would essentially constitute full academic dress. Additionally, the majority of the choir are undergraduates, who may not have any entitlement to wear a hood
St Peter's	Dark suits, white shirts and the green college tie (men); All black or black bottoms and white tops (women), with flexibility for those who may not conform to that binary	Does not wear a hood	Have never been asked to wear hoods, but would be largely incompatible with dress code
Somerville	Concert blacks with gowns	Does not wear a hood	Not permitted to wear hoods, as the dress code is incompatible
University	Smart clothes with gowns	Does not wear a hood	Not permitted to wear hoods
Worcester	Cassocks and surplices	Will often wear a hood[3]	Wearing of hoods is permitted

3   There has recently been a high turnover of directors at Worcester, with a new permanent Director of Chapel Music appointed to begin in Michaelmas Term 2023.

the University Church (admittedly, not an Oxford collegiate choir) was awaiting the arrival of cassocks, having simply worn surplices over normal clothing in the past, as a direct result of comments from livestreams, and the desire for a tidy and uniform presentation of the ensemble. The arrival of the cassocks for the 2023/4 academic year has forestalled further such comments.

The lack of uniformity, or perception thereof, seems to be intrinsically linked with the opposition on the grounds of elitism. Once again, one can perhaps understand this opposition, as the wearing of an academic hood is a visible indicator of achievement. However, disregarding the politics of hood-wearing in other settings displaying one's academic status in a collegiate choir would seem to be an appropriate practice, not least because every member of the institution will, presumably, one day be entitled to wear an academic hood themselves.

The final ground for opposition—that the wearing of hoods is a distraction from worship—is the one which would seemingly bear the least weight. As shown above, canon law, until the most recent revision, stated quite clearly that both clergy and choir (where entitled) should wear academic hoods. Therefore, one might resolve that the wearing of academic hoods, when stipulated, is both a necessity and an integral part of worship. It should, however, be considered that uniformity once again comes into play here. It is held by some that the purpose of liturgical dress is to make everyone equal, and that wearing an academic hood would make one stand out as a result. One can appreciate this stance, but can counter that hoods may be worn by members of the clergy: if it is permitted for them (and acceptable in a theologically democratic aesthetic), then why not for members of a choir?

At this juncture of the inquiry, one can see that the of wearing academic hoods in Oxford collegiate choirs is very much a continuing tradition, with half of the colleges in question promoting a culture of hood-wearing without any barriers to awarding institution. However, this culture is mixed, and does often pivot on the discretion of whoever has authority to decide whether or not hood-wearing will be permitted. Various oppositions, as seen above, play into these decisions, with arguments of uniformity tending to win out in the established choral foundations.

Contemporary attitudes of members of collegiate choirs

Aside from the raw data about the collegiate choirs which admit members via the choral and organ awards, as given above, the consultation with those who actually live the tradition—in this instance, the members of each of these choirs—is essential to the understanding of contemporary practice.

The questionnaire which was devised and circulated to members of the collegiate choir community in Oxford from October to December 2022, consisted of the following questions.

1. To which College Choir do you belong?
2. What base dress code does your choir have for services?
3. Does your choir permit the wearing of hoods?
4. Are you entitled to wear any kind of academic hood? (Including those from the RCO, ABRSM, TCL or similar institutions)?
   a. [*If 'Yes' to 4.*] Which hood(s) are you entitled to wear? (Name the degree/award)

b. Do you wear this hood in service? (/would you wear it if you were allowed?)

5. [*If 'No' to 4.*] Would you wear a hood if you were entitled to do so?

6. If you answered 'sometimes' [*in response to 4b. or 5.*], please explain the occasions for which you would wear a hood.

7. What is your opinion towards the wearing of academic hoods in a collegiate choir setting? (Please explain your stance, be it aesthetic, theological, liturgical, etc.)

8. Do you wish to add anything further concerning the wearing of academic hoods in a collegiate choir setting?

The 66 responses draw an interesting picture of attitudes across the 16 college choirs included in this work.[34] The dress codes (perhaps unsurprisingly) correspond with the information given by the Organists/Directors of each ensemble. In response to question 4, a large array of hoods was cited, with a particular abundance of hoods awarded for degrees from Oxford. The specific hoods cited are as follows:

BA (Oxon)	MEng (Cantab)	LTCL
MA (Oxon)	LLM (Cantab)	LRSM
BTh (Oxon)	BA (Dunelm)	DipABRSM
MMath (Oxon)	LLB (Dub)	ARCO
BCL (Oxon)	MEd (Chichester)	
MSt (Oxon)		
MPhil (Oxon)		

Whilst the abundance of Oxford and Cambridge (over half of the responses) is not surprising, attention should be drawn to the third column. These represent hoods for non-degree awards, and confirm the suspicion, above, that many undergraduates coming into the collegiate choirs may well be entitled to wear an academic hood though they are yet to have been awarded a degree. Further analysis shows a marked lack of first degrees within the mix, with only the Oxford and Durham Bachelor of Arts, Oxford Bachelor of Theology, Oxford Master of Mathematics (a four-year first degree) and Trinity Dublin Bachelor of Law, the remaining seven represent six higher postgraduate degrees and the Oxford Master of Arts (which is a change of status conferred to those eligible upon application).

There were two erroneous responses to this question, from one respondent clearly not a current member of any of the collegiate choirs (their whole response was not used for the purposes of the data) which listed hoods of an Associate of the Royal Schools of Church Music and a Fellow of the Guildhall School of Music—one would expect both to be beyond the reach of even the most accomplished postgraduate student.

When compared to the responses from the Organists/Directors of Music, what is interesting is the larger degree of support towards the wearing of academic hoods in the setting of an Oxford collegiate choir, regardless of whether the rules of the choir actually permit it (see Table 3).

---

34 There were 67 respondents in total, representing the colleges as follows: Brasenose (2), Christ Church (5), Exeter (3), Harris Manchester (1), Keble (7), Magdalen (9), Merton (6), New (2), Oriel (4), Pembroke (2), Queen's (13), Somerville (3), St Edmund Hall (2), St Peter's (2), University (1), Worcester (4), and one (1) ineligible respondent.

Table 3. Support for wearing of hoods in collegiate choirs, collected from members of eligible choirs in October–December 2022. (Figures rounded.) *n* = 66

63%	27%	12%
Yes	No	N/a

The statistics for complete support broadly match the data gathered above (with 50 per cent of the choirs allowing hoods compared to the 61 per cent support from responding members) but when one accounts for the reasonable portion of respondents who stated that they had no opinion either way, this results in only a 27 per cent complete opposition to the wearing of hoods in a collegiate setting. This should, however, be caveated with the fact that many respondents in support of the wearing of hoods stated that they would reserve this for particular occasions of importance, including Sundays, feast days, and major college services/events. This usage would seem to depend on the college choir, and the culture of use within each.

To address the opposition to the wearing of hoods from this questionnaire, we may once again return to the categories of opposition which were defined above:

1. Incompatibility with base dress code (i.e., gowns)
2. Lack of uniformity/promotes elitism
3. Distraction from worship

It should be immediately noted that the first category of opposition—incompatibility with dress code—does not feature at all within the responses. This is unsurprising, as one would expect that particular opposition to lie exclusively with whoever is in charge of setting the base dress code; the members of the choirs would not concern themselves with that particular aspect of the argument. What may be deemed more interesting, however, is the fact that the number of respondents who simply did not understand what or why academic hoods may be worn (referred to as 'Other' in Table 4) is directly matched by the number of respondents who opposed the wearing of hoods for reasons of distraction from worship. The lack of opposition on the grounds of distraction from worship reinforces the sentiment above; that being the wearing of academic hoods is broadly accepted as a normal (and perhaps, required) part of worship, despite any impacts it may have on a theologically democratic aesthetic.

The largest degree of opposition to the practice of hood-wearing is clearly on the grounds of uniformity and/or elitism. These two are, once again, intertwined—with

Table 4. Reasons for opposition towards wearing academic hoods, collected from current members of eligible choirs in October–December 2022. *n* = 66

78%		11%	11%
Uniformity/elitism	*(Incompatibility: 0%)*	Distraction from worship	Other

the lack of uniformity seemingly leading inevitably to a creation of an elitist hierarchy within the choir. It is, perhaps, worth noting that of those who opposed on the grounds of uniformity/elitism, only 29 per cent were entitled to wear a hood—an opinion which might well alter once this entitlement changes (which, at least anecdotally, tends to be the case). Whatever the case, as discussed above, the lack of uniformity created by the wearing of hoods is well within the bounds of what is allowed by canon law, as well as a practice echoed by the clergy, before considering the academic nature of the setting of a collegiate chapel.

Conclusions

As has been seen, the wearing of academic hoods as part of the liturgical dress of a choir member is permitted in so far as canon law is concerned and can trace its roots back to the earliest documents of the Church of England. The sources of guidance for the wearing of academic dress in the University of Oxford show that the requirement to wear an academic hood itself is limited to a small handful of events, and it has been explained that the overlap these have with any need for choirs to be in liturgical dress is minute. The University did relax its own rules concerning the wearing of another institution's academic dress, but this, again, has little bearing on the use of hoods in collegiate chapels, other than perhaps providing a legitimate argument for the wearing of non-Oxford hoods in those college choirs which rigorously uphold that restriction.

The two-stage approach of the inquiry allowed for a detailed, overarching view of the tradition of hood-wearing in Oxford collegiate choirs. From the data collected from the Organists/Directors of Music, three main areas of opposition towards the wearing of hoods in a collegiate setting were identified: an incompatibility with base dress code; a lack of uniformity and/or the culture promotes elitism; and that the wearing can be a distraction from worship. Whilst the roots of these three oppositions are understandable, it has been shown that they bear little weight under interrogation.

The responses from current members of the collegiate institutions illustrate an interesting picture in themselves, indicating a large majority in support, with a little over a quarter of respondents actively opposing the practice. Additionally, when the reasons for this opposition are explored, most respondents based their complaints on the lack of uniformity and/or fostering an attitude of elitism, which would seem to ignore both the practice of hood-wearing for the clergy, as well as the very environment of an Oxford collegiate chapel (that being an academic one).

It is clear that the practice of hood-wearing in the collegiate choirs of the University of Oxford remains active, despite constantly shifting. On the whole, the evidence presented in this article shows that attitudes are in support of the tradition.

Acknowledgement

Photos from the Burgon Society Archive by Chris Williams.

Transactions of the Burgon Society, 23 (2023), pages 110–128

An Odd Habit: A Study of the Use of the Academic Hood in the Portraits of the Archbishops of Armagh

By Peter A. Thompson

The city of Armagh, or as it is known in the Irish tongue, *Ard Mhacha* (the high place of Macha, or Macha's height), is the ecclesiastical capital of Ireland. It was on the hill of Ard Mhacha that Saint Patrick founded his 'great church' in the middle years of the fifth century (traditionally dated to 445 AD) and the old legends record that the saint decreed that this church should have preeminence over all of the churches in Ireland forever. Whether the legend is true, or a later creation to support Armagh's claim to the primacy, it has been and remains the seat of the successors of St Patrick, firstly the abbots, then bishops, and from 1106 AD archbishops of Armagh, a continuous succession from Patrick to the present day. There are two cathedrals dedicated to the saint in the city. The Church of Ireland (Anglican) Cathedral of St Patrick is on the hill of Armagh, the site of the fifth century church, and the Roman Catholic Cathedral sits on one of the surrounding hills.

Church House (Armagh) is situated on the hill of Armagh, beside the See House, and opposite the Cathedral and the Armagh Robinson Library, demarcating the Cathedral Close. The Primate Alexander Synod Hall is on the first floor of the building. The foundation stone of the Synod Hall was laid in 1911 and it was opened in 1913. Although built primarily as a venue for the annual diocesan synod of the diocese of Armagh, it functions as a space for large diocesan gatherings and also as a 'parish hall' for the cathedral. Refreshments after major diocesan, provincial and national events are served in the Synod Hall, and it has been used during the renovation of the Cathedral building for the regular daily and weekly services for the Cathedral congregation.

The offices of the diocesan administration are on the ground floor, as are other meeting rooms, including the Council Room, where regular meetings of the diocesan council and committees are held. During the Covid-19 pandemic (as a result of the need for increased social distancing) many of these smaller meetings were held upstairs in the Synod Hall, and during numerous tedious sessions I found my mind drawn more to the episcopal portraits hanging on the walls than the agenda under discussion. The changing fashions in episcopal dress and wigs were fascinating, but beyond a general interest it was obvious that there was a considerable period of time when the use of the academic hood with episcopal habit was considered normative, and that observation sowed the seeds of this article.

The issues around the wearing of academic hoods 'in quire' have been dealt with thoroughly by the late Nicholas Groves, whose paper in *Transactions of the Burgon Society*[1] considers history, practice, canon law and common misconceptions around the

---

1 'The Use of the Academic Hood in Quire', *TBS*, 8 (2008), pp. 98–105.

Fig. 1. St Patrick's Cathedral, Armagh.

Fig. 2. Church House, Armagh.

use of the hood. While focused primarily on musicians, it also covers the requirements and traditional use of the hood by clergy, but not specifically by bishops. In *Theological Colleges: Their Hoods and Histories*,[2] Groves gives some further information on the history and use of hoods by the clergy. This article is an attempt to build upon those sources, using as a foundation the portrait collection of the archbishops of Armagh as evidence of evolving custom and historical practice. The initial questions are what was worn, and when, thus an initial survey of the portraits will attempt to identify both the particular hoods worn, and the time period in which their use was normative. The results of this raise a secondary, often contentious, question, of whether the hood should be worn with the chimere—or not?[3] The initial survey will establish that for a period of over a century there is clear evidence of all archbishops choosing to wear their hoods over a chimere. Some comments on the origins of the chimere will then attempt to address the question from a historical perspective, thus drawing together both custom and practice across the centuries.

The terms rochet and chimere have multiple meanings, or to be more precise the garments exist in multiple (related but distinct) forms. Throughout this paper the terms are always used with reference to the classic Anglican form unless otherwise indicated. The rochet is a long white garment, similar in form to the Surplice, but with narrower sleeves, gathered at the cuff by a coloured band forming a ruffle. It is a traditional part of episcopal choir dress. The chimere is descended from a riding cloak, and is similar in appearance to a sleeveless academic gown. It is worn over the rochet, and is traditionally black or scarlet.

Several limitations to the extent of this article should be noted. Firstly it relates only to one diocese of one member Church of the Anglican Communion. A similar exercise in other dioceses and/or provinces would serve either to confirm or to challenge the general hypothesis that the use of the hood can be sanctioned by custom over an

---

2   London: Burgon Society, 2004.

3   Janet Mayo states boldly (and without any sources or references) that 'the bishop should never wear an academic hood with either the red or black chimere.' (*A History of Ecclesiastical Dress* (London: Batsford, 1984), p. 120.)

extended period.[4] Secondly it is a collection of formal portraits, where, it might be expected, a particularly formal and conservative choice of dress would be exercised. There is some photographic and anecdotal evidence from more recent years which could enlarge the evidence in relation to customary use. Thirdly, 'it is worth bearing in mind that artists' representations of dress should be approached critically,'[5] hence the somewhat cautious appraisal of certain features and details, for example the McCann portrait.

The portraits

There are some thirty-two[6] portraits in the collection, beginning with Adam Loftus, who became primate in 1563, and chronologically complete from Henry Ussher (who became archbishop and primate in 1595) to the present day. The most recent portrait, that of Archbishop Richard Clarke, was added in December 2022, following his retirement in February 2020.

The collection is a remarkable repository of information in many areas, not least of clerical dress and contemporary fashion. The large ruffs of Henry Ussher (1595) and his successors give way to a flat shoulder covering[7] in the time of John Bramhall (1661), which in turn reduces to the more recognizable preaching bands by the time of Narcissus Marsh (1703). The same three archbishops also see the fashion changing from short cropped hair with a skull cap, to long curled hair, and finally to the clerical wig, a fashion only abandoned by Lord John George Beresford in 1822. The beards of the late sixteenth and early seventeenth centuries disappeared for over two hundred years, not reappearing until the early twentieth century. While the rochet and (black) chimere were *de rigueur* in all of the early portraits, to that was added the jewel of the prelate of the Order of St Patrick by Archbishop Stuart (1800–22) and several of his successors. Archbishop Marcus Gervais Beresford[8] further added the mantle of the Order.

Fig. 3. The interior of the Synod Hall, showing some of the portrait collection.

The first archbishop to be pictured wearing a hood was Archbishop Knox, who succeeded Marcus Beresford in 1886, and the fashion continued without exception for

---

4   There are several episcopal portraits from the diocese of Clogher in C. Costecalde and B. Walker (eds), *The Church of Ireland, An Illustrated History* (Dublin: Booklink, n.d.), pp. 140–44, which confirm the findings of this article.

5   A. Ribeiro, 'Truth and Imagination: How Real Is Dress in Art?', *Journal of Dress History*, 1.1 (2017), pp. 3–5.

6   The total rises to thirty-four if the portrait of Mrs Alexander, and the second portrait of Archbishop Richard Robinson which is on loan to the Armagh Observatory are both included.

7   This was a turned-down collar, known at the time as a 'falling band'.

8   Marcus Gervais Beresford was archbishop in 1862–85. His predecessor was his first cousin once removed, Lord John George de la Poer Beresford (who was archbishop from 1822 until 1862). Marcus' father was Bishop George de la Poer Beresford, bishop of Kilmore (1802–39), who was a nephew of William Beresford, 1st Baron Decies and archbishop of Tuam (1794–1819).

120 years, the pattern only broken by Archbishop Harper who was elected in 2007. We will now examine briefly each of the 'hooded' portraits.

Robert Bent Knox (1808–93) is the first of the primates to wear a hood in his portrait. He was archbishop of Armagh from 1886 to 1893, having previously been consecrated as bishop for the united dioceses of Down, Connor and Dromore in 1849, and before that serving in the dioceses of Limerick and Kilmore. He held the degrees of BA (1829), MA (1834), BD and DD (1858) from Trinity College Dublin,[9] and LLD Cantab (1888).[10]

The hood in the portrait (Fig. 4) is unclear, exhibiting a reasonably wide red neckband, unbound. His left shoulder appears to reveal a black lining, suggesting the DD hood. While the Dublin hoods are customarily bound on the neckband and cape, there are numerous examples where both are unbound. Within the archive of the Burgon Society[11] are a number of Dublin hoods. WBS-244 shows a standard MusB, while WBS-448 is another hood of the same shape, but unbound. The date ascribed is *c.* 1930s. WBS-407 is a standard DD, bound on the neckband and cape, while WPG-034 is unbound on both. These two examples serve to illustrate the regular deviation from the norm.

The 1972 edition of Frank Haycraft's *Degrees and Hoods* adds a curious comment to the Dublin entry. It says: 'all hoods of this University are of a

Fig. 4. Archbishop Knox, by Emily C. Way (1893).

special full shape. Nowadays they are edged by extending the silk lining but this was a tailor's innovation and any graduate may have his hood made without this edging, so greatly improving the appearance.'[12] No other volume on academic dress contains a comparable note, and it may be sheer speculation to ask is this an editorial addition by Franklyn.

Robert Samuel Gregg (1834–96) was archbishop from 1893 to 1896. He was consecrated as bishop in 1875 for Cork, Cloyne and Ross, succeeding his father in that see. Previously he had served in the dioceses of Cork and Connor, having been at one time chaplain to his father. He held the degrees of BA (1857), MA (1860), BD and DD (1873) from Trinity College Dublin.[13]

---

9 Full details of the scheme of academic dress in Trinity (more precisely the University of Dublin, of which Trinity is the only constituent college, and thus is used interchangeably) can be found in Nicholas Groves, (ed.), *Shaw's Academical Dress*, 3rd edn (London: Burgon Society, 2011), pp. 145–48. That of Oxford may be found on pp. 320–23, and Cambridge on pp. 110–14.

10 Biographical details from W. E. C. Fleming, *Armagh Clergy 1800–2000* (Dundalk: Dundalgan Press, 2001), pp. 40–41.

11 At <burgon.org.uk/archive/british-and-irish-collection> [retrieved 28 June 2024].

12 Frank W. Haycraft, *The Degrees and Hoods of the World's Universities and Colleges*, 5th edn, ed. by Frederick R. Rogers, Charles A. H. Franklyn, George W. Shaw and Hugh Alexander Boyd (Lewes: Baxter, 1972), p. 28.

13 Biographical details from Fleming, pp. 42–43.

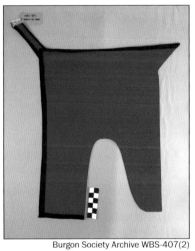

Fig. 5. Dublin DD (bound).

Fig. 6. Dublin DD (bound).

Fig. 7. Dublin DD (unbound).

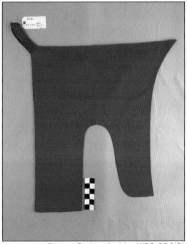

Fig. 8. Dublin DD (unbound).

Photos by Chris Williams

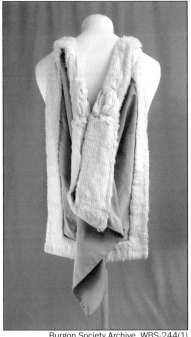

Fig. 9. Dublin MusB (bound).

Fig. 10. Dublin MusB (unbound).

Fig. 11. Archbishop R. S. Gregg,
English School, late 19th century (1894).

Fig. 12. Archbishop Alexander,
by Walter Frederick Osborne
(1893).

Fig. 13. Archbishop Crozier by
Frederick Whiting (1911).

Fig. 14. Archbishop Crozier by
Mark Milbanke (1920).

His portrait (Fig. 11) depicts a much narrower red neckband bound with black, clearly the hood of a Dublin Doctor of Divinity.

William Alexander (1824–1911) was the husband of the well-known hymn writer Cecil Frances Alexander.[14] He succeeded Gregg to the primacy and was archbishop from 1896 to 1911. He was consecrated in 1867 for the see of Derry, in which diocese he had served all his early ministry apart from a short spell as dean of Emly (a sinecure). He held degrees from Oxford: BA (1850), MA (1857), DD (1867), DCL (1876), DLitt (1907), and Dublin: LLD (1892).[15]

The Alexander portrait (Fig. 12) shows just a narrow red neckband, possibly bound in pink, suggesting the Dublin doctorate.[16] The insurance valuation of this portrait ascribes a date of 1893, so this is just possible.[17] A second portrait of Alexander hangs in the dining room, showing a hood with grey lining, presumably the Oxford DLitt.

John Baptist Crozier (1853–1920) was primate from 1911 to 1920. He was consecrated in 1897 as bishop of Ossory, Ferns and Leighlin, and translated to Down, Connor and Dromore in 1907. His early ministry was spent in the dioceses of Connor and of Down. His degrees were all from Dublin: BA (1872), MA (1875), BD and DD (1888).[18]

---

14 Famous for hymns including 'Once in Royal David's City', 'There Is a Green Hill Far Away' and 'All Things Bright and Beautiful', amongst others.

15 Biographical details from Fleming, pp. 44–45.

16 A portion of the 1910 portrait is visible at <www.stpatricks-cathedral.org/people /abbots-bishops-archbishops/> [retrieved 1 July 2024]. It was painted by Harry R. Douglas, who was also commissioned to paint a portrait of Bishop William Pakenham Walsh, which currently hangs in the music room at Christ Church Cathedral, Dublin. The bishop is wearing a Dublin DD hood over a black chimere, adding further evidence that this was normative practice.

17 Danny Kinahan, 'Valuation for insurance purposes', a formal appraisal document in the diocesan office.

18 Biographical details from Fleming, pp. 46–47.

Fig. 15. Archbishop D'Arcy, by Frederick Whiting (1920).

Fig. 16. Archbishop D'Arcy, by Sir John Lavery (1928).

Ulster Museum

The hood in his portrait (Fig. 13) is clearly the Dublin DD, a scarlet neckband, bound black. Like Alexander, Crozier has a second portrait in the dining room (Fig. 14), the earliest example of a scarlet chimere and hood, again clearly the Dublin DD, worn rather nonchalantly over the shoulder. Archbishop Crozier is the first archbishop who is clearly wearing an episcopal ring.

Charles Frederick D'Arcy (1859–1938) was consecrated as bishop of Clogher in 1903, translated to Ossory, Ferns and Leighlin in 1907, to Down Connor and Dromore in 1911, to Dublin in August 1919 and less than a year later to Armagh in June 1920. His early ministry was spent between the dioceses of Down and Connor. He graduated from Trinity College Dublin as follows: BA (1882), MA (1889), BD (1892), DD (1900) and LittD (1934). He was an HonDD of Oxford (1920), the Queen's University of Belfast (1929), and the University of Glasgow.[19] He is one of only two archbishops to have been so honoured by QUB.[20]

Frustratingly, the Whiting portrait (Fig. 15) exhibits only a plain red neckband perhaps indicating the Oxford degree, although as noted above unbound neckbands are not unknown in Dublin. This portrait is dated 1920, the year the Oxford degree was awarded. There is, however, another portrait of Archbishop D'Arcy, by Sir John

---

19 This later degree is recorded in the *Dictionary of Irish Biography* but not in Fleming.
20 Biographical details from Fleming, pp. 48–49.

National Museums NI

Fig. 17. Portrait of an Unidentified Cleric, by William Conor (1881–1968).

Fig. 18. Archbishop Day, by Sir Oswald Birley.

Fig. 19. Archbishop J. A. F. Gregg, by Frank McKelvey (1939).

Lavery, in the Ulster Museum.[21] In this portrait he is wearing a scarlet hood with a similar neckband as the portrait above, which appears to be lined black and unbound. The shape of the neckband and the slight curvature at the base of the cape are suggestive of the Oxford DD, through not conclusive. A third portrait has come to light, described as 'Portrait of an Unidentified Cleric' in the collection of the National Museums of Northern Ireland (Fig. 17). The portrait is by William Connor, and clearly depicted Archbishop D'Arcy. He is wearing the gown of a Doctor of Divinity, which could be either that of Dublin or Oxford.

John Godfrey Fitzmaurice Day was elected by the House of Bishops 'ad interim' bishop of Armagh on 15 June 1920, the Armagh Synod having failed to elect a new primate, and appointed to the vacant bishopric of Ossory, Ferns and Leighlin in September 1920. In 1938 the House of Bishops again elected him, this time to the vacant see of Armagh. He was elected on 27 April, enthroned on 9 June, and after only a few days in Armagh he went for surgery and died in a Dublin nursing home on 26 September. He was a Cambridge man, graduating BA (1896) and MA (1902). He was awarded

21 At <artuk.org/discover/artworks/most-reverend-charles-frederick-darcy-18591938-ma-dd-archbishop-of-armagh-and-primate-of-all-ireland-122359> [retrieved 28 June 2024].

118

a Dublin DD *jure dignitatis* (1920), and an additional DD from King's College, Nova Scotia (1937).[22]

Once again the portrait (Fig. 18) only exhibits a plain red neckband (unbound). Given the fact that he was awarded the Canadian degree before his translation to Armagh, and that the portrait is most likely from the time of his translation, it is possible that the hood is for either degree. The tradition in Nova Scotia is to follow the Oxford system of academic dress.[23]

John Allen Fitzgerald Gregg (1873–1961) was a grandson of Bishop Gregg of Cork, and a nephew of Archbishop Robert Samuel Gregg (above) of Armagh. After appointments in Connor and Cork and an academic appointment in Dublin (Archbishop King's Professor of Divinity, TCD, 1911–15), he was consecrated in 1915 for the dioceses of Ossory, Ferns and Leighlin. In 1920 the House of Bishops elected him archbishop of Dublin, and in 1938 they again elected him this time to succeed Archbishop Day in Armagh. He was enthroned in January 1939, and was the first archbishop to retire, in 1959 (at the age of 86). He is one of a very small number of people to be awarded the degree of DD by the Queen's University of Belfast, and the second and last archbishop of the Church of Ireland to be so honoured. He graduated from Cambridge: BA (1894), MA (1898), BD (1909), DD (1939); Dublin: BD *ad eundem* (1911), DD (1913); and QUB: DD (1949).[24]

The lining of his hood (Fig. 19) is unclear; much seems to be in the shadows, but there is just enough silk to show it is the Cambridge DD (turquoise shot rose), uniquely an earned DD (for work on John's gospel). Gregg habitually wore his Dublin hood until he received the Cambridge degree. In retirement he gave away his Dublin robes, and the gown is now in the collection of the Burgon Society. Archbishop Gregg is the first of the archbishops to wear a pectoral cross in his portrait.

James McCann (1897–1983) was elected and consecrated bishop of Meath in 1945, following a series of clerical appointments in Connor, Kilmore and Meath dioceses. He was elected as primate in 1959, and served for just over ten years, retiring in 1969. He is the first Belfast graduate to become primate, and the first primate to have earned a PhD. He initially studied in QUB, where he graduated BA in 1919. He received the following degrees from TCD: BA (1926), MA (1930), BD (1935), PhD (1944), DD *jure dignitatis* (1945), LLD (1966).[25]

For his portrait Archbishop McCann chose to wear his PhD hood, presumably as his highest examined degree rather than a degree he had received as a result of his office.[26] The painter appears to have taken some licence, adding a gold lining to his chimere, but the hood is unmistakable.[27] The comment by Ribeiro, noted in the intro-

---

22 Biographical details from Fleming, pp. 50–51

23 See John N. Grant, 'Many Coloured Coats: The Systems of Academical Dress in Nova Scotian Universities', *TBS*, 9 (2009), pp. 183–99.

24 Biographical details from Fleming, pp. 52–54.

25 Biographical details from Fleming, p. 55.

26 A portion of the 1959 portrait is visible at <www.stpatricks-cathedral.org/people /abbots-bishops-archbishops/> [retrieved 1 July 2024].

27 An Oxford Convocation habit is part-lined with the silk used to line the hood. The Dublin PhD hood is lined yellow.

Fig. 20. Arch-
bishop Simms,
by Basil Black-
shaw (1969).

© Victor Patterson, Images4Media

Fig. 21. Archbishop Simms, DLitt (New University
of Ulster).

L. Whiteside, *George Otto Simms; A Biography*

Fig. 22. At the Anglican Congress in Toronto, 1963. Archbishop Simms in the Dublin (or
Huron?) DD.

L. Whiteside, *George Otto Simms; A Biography*

Fig. 23. Lam-
beth Confer-
ence 1978,
conferring of
DCL from the
University of
Kent.

duction, is worthy of repetition at this point: 'it is worth bearing in mind that artists' representations of dress should be approached critically.'[28] It is likely that this is the artist's attempt to add some shade and character to the portrait, and unlikely that to be a true representation of the chimere worn.

George Otto Simms (1910–91) served a three-year curacy in Dublin followed by a year as chaplain to Lincoln Theological College, thirteen years as dean of residence and lecturer at Trinity College Dublin, and a number of months as dean of Cork before being elected and consecrated bishop of Cork, Cloyne and Ross in 1952. In 1956 he was elected archbishop of Dublin, and in 1969 the House of Bishops chose him as archbishop of Armagh. He retired in 1980. He graduated from Dublin as BA (1932), MA (1935), BD (1936), PhD (1950), and DD *jure dignitatis* (1952). He was

© ITV

Fig. 24. Archbishop Simms, wearing the Huron DD, General Synod 1965.

awarded a DD from Huron (1963) and a DCL from the University of Kent at Canterbury (1978).[29] Although not recorded by Fleming, he was also awarded a DLitt by the New University of Ulster, which has a tradition of gifting a hood to honorary graduates, and he was seen in this hood periodically (Fig. 21).

The detail of Archbishop Simms' portrait (Fig. 20) is frustratingly unclear. The neckband could be plain red, although there does seem to be a very fine gold binding, suggestive of his PhD. On balance it seems more likely that this is the brown or buff colour used by the artist to highlight folds in the material, as on his scarf. A small area of his right shoulder seems to have black binding, which would indicate DD, which on balance of probability is most likely. The subject's right shoulder is much less defined, but this might be for compositional reasons.

John Ward Armstrong (1915–87) spent the first thirty years of his ordained ministry in various appointments in the diocese of Dublin, culminating in the deanery of the National Cathedral (St Patrick's, Dublin). He was elected and consecrated as bishop of Cashel and Emly, Waterford and Lismore in 1968, and subsequently appointed bishop of the united dioceses of Cashel, Waterford, Lismore, Ossory, Ferns and Leighlin in 1977. The House of Bishops elected him to the primacy in 1980, and he retired in 1986. His degrees were all from Trinity College Dublin: BA (1938), BD (1945), MA (1957), and DD *jure dignitatis* (1981).[30]

Armstrong is the first primate who was not awarded a DD *jure dignitatis* on his consecration as a bishop, it being awarded on his translation to the primacy. He was also the last primate to be awarded the degree *jure dignitatis* by Trinity. His portrait shows a plain red neckband, presumably the DD as this was his only scarlet hood, though it is more customarily bound black.[31]

---

28 Aileen Ribeiro, 'Truth and Imagination: How Real Is Dress in Art?', *The Journal of Dress History*, 1.1 (2017), pp. 3–5.

29 Biographical details from Fleming, pp. 56–57.

30 Biographical details from Fleming, pp. 58–59.

31 A portion of the 1980 portrait is visible at <www.stpatricks-cathedral.org/people/abbots-bishops-archbishops/> [retrieved 1 July 2024].

Robert Henry Alexander Eames, OM, Baron Eames of Armagh (b. 1937) spent his entire priestly ministry in the diocese of Down. He was elected and consecrated bishop of Derry and Raphoe in 1975, translated to Down and Dromore in 1980, and to Armagh in 1986. He graduated from QUB: LLB (1960), PhD (1963), and LLD *honoris causa* (1989). He was awarded many doctorates *honoris causa*, including TCD LLD (1992), Greenwich University School of Theology DLitt (1993), Cambridge DD (1994), Lancaster LLD (1994), Aberdeen DD (1997), Exeter DD (1999), Ulster LLD (2002), London DD (2008).[32] The portrait of Archbishop Eames shows a pale blue binding on a scarlet hood, with a hint of pink lining, which is the QUB LLD.[33]

The Church of Ireland, an Illustrated History

Fig. 25. Archbishop Eames.

The wearing of hoods ceased with the appointment of Archbishop Alan Edwin Thomas Harper, who was archbishop from 2007 until 2012. He was the first archbishop not to hold a doctoral degree—neither earned, *honoris causa* nor *jure dignitatis*. He is a graduate of the University of Leeds (BA), and prior to his consecration as bishop of Connor regularly wore the distinctive Leeds green hood. Towards the end of his tenure as archbishop he was awarded an HonDD from a seminary in the United States, though he never disclosed any further details.

He was succeeded by Richard Lionel Clarke who held office from 2012 to 2020. He was a graduate of Trinity (BA, PhD) and London (BD), but again followed his predecessor's fashion in eschewing the hood. Before his elevation to the primacy, as bishop of Meath and Kildare, he was seen regularly in his PhD hood. The current primate, Francis John McDowell is a graduate of Belfast (BA) and Dublin (BTh). His portrait will not be commissioned until his retirement but thus far a hood has never been worn, and it seems that this particular fashion has reached its end, at least for the present moment, in the see of Armagh.

Canon Law

Until the disestablishment of the Church of Ireland in 1871 the Irish Church was subject to English canon law. Post-disestablishment the Church of Ireland was responsible for its own canon law, and introduced a series of harshly anti-ritualistic canons. Curiously, there is no guidance given to episcopal vesture in the canon law of the Church of Ireland. For those unfamiliar with the history and practice of the Church of Ireland, the relevant portion of the current Canon 12,[34] 'Ecclesiastical Apparel', says:

> (1) Archbishops and bishops at all times of their public ministration of the services of the Church shall use the customary ecclesiastical apparel of their order.[35]

It continues to require the wearing of a surplice and a scarf or stole by the clergy, with the cassock, bands and hood listed as optional. The black gown may be worn when

32 Biographical details from Fleming, pp. 60–61.

33 A portion of the 1986 portrait is visible at <www.stpatricks-cathedral.org/people/abbots-bishops-archbishops/> [retrieved 1 July 2024].

34 The current canons were updated in the 1970s to permit the use of coloured stoles.

35 B. M. H. Shiel (ed.), *The Constitution of the Church of Ireland*, amended 2021 (Dublin, General Synod of the Church of Ireland, 2003).

preaching, and 'no other vestment or ornament' is permitted. No doctrinal significance is attached to the variety of vesture permitted.

These are the current canons, which have now been in place since 1972. Before that point the use of the stole was not permitted, and so traditional choir dress (including the hood) was the norm.

It is interesting that the single sentence referring to those in episcopal orders is one of the most vaguely worded paragraphs in the *Constitution of the Church of Ireland*. What does the word 'customary' mean in this case? Reading these from a strictly legal standpoint (for how else can canon law be read?) there are perhaps three different interpretations which can be advanced as lawful. One is that customary refers to the episcopal order, as it has existed for almost two millennia. A second is that it refers to the custom of the Anglican family of churches or indeed the Church of England since the time it declared autonomy from Rome in the sixteenth century. A third interpretation is more parochial again, defining customary as what had become customary in the Church of Ireland at the time of disestablishment in the late nineteenth century, when the original canons were framed. Whichever interpretation is accepted, none gives any further assistance on the question of the correctness of wearing a hood over a chimere.

This raises a further question of how long does it take for practice to become customary. Over the four centuries covered in this portrait collection it is clear that practice has evolved, for example the preference for the black chimere giving way to the scarlet (during the episcopates of Archbishops Crozier and D'Arcy), the use of the clerical wig (1703–1822), the addition of the jewel (and later the mantle) of the Order of St Patrick (1822, 1862), the introduction of the episcopal ring (Archbishop Crozier) and pectoral cross (Archbishop Gregg), and the use of the hood. What this collection cannot tell us is what was worn on a regular basis, but it is worthy of note that what was seen as normative for a formal portrait sets a tone for general standards of vesture.

The chimere and hood — an odd habit?

We have established the customary use of the hood with the chimere over an extended period, and now we shall turn to the origins of the chimere to see if any further light may be shed on the historical basis for this custom.

Herbert Norris defines the chimere as:

> ... a short sleeveless cloak, or coat of sheepskin of Spanish origin ... called the 'zamarra'. This is the origin of the garment known as the simar, worn by royalty and gentry at the end of the fifteenth and during the sixteenth century. Also of the 'chamarre' ... This is an old French word. And both it and the Spanish zamarra derive ultimately from the same root, from which we obtain the English term chimere.[36]

Norris then traces the origin of the chimere from the twelfth century and states that it was worn by bishops of the Western church as an outdoor garment, for riding and other purposes, but not as a liturgical vestment. He further asserts that it was made at first of black silk, and later in various colours, lined for warmth. He reproduces an im-

36 *Church Vestments; Their Origin and Development* (New York: Dover, 2002), p. 177. Norris, Robinson and others recognize that there are two distinct garments which have been referred to as a 'chimere', but for the purposes of this article we will exclude the garment worn under the rochet, and focus on the common understanding of the word today. For details on the *simar*, see Norris's *Costume and Fashion*, Vol. III, pp. 18–19.

age of the twelfth century archbishop, Stephen Langton, wearing a chimere of purple silk over a scarlet cassock and white rochet, and over the shoulders a hood of scarlet lined with white (Fig. 26).

From the fourteenth century he reproduces another similar plate of a bishop in cassock, rochet, chimere, hood and pileus.

Fig. 26. Archbishop Langton, reproduced from Norris.

In her book on medieval costume, Mary G. Houston makes no reference to the chimere.[37] The discussion on clerical costume focuses primarily on the Eucharistic vestments and monastic habits, making little reference to vesture for the offices, and none to the outdoor dress of the clergy. The discussion on academic dress in the fifteenth century observes the use of the *taberdum*, the *cappa clausa*, the *pallium* (not to be confused with the archiepiscopal *pallium*) and the *super-pellicum*. This lack of reference to the chimere as either clerical or academic supports Norris's belief that its origins are as an outdoor garment.

N. F. Robinson looks to establish a common ancestry in the chimere and the various types of academic habit identified by Houston. He refutes the suggestion that the chimere is a form of the *cappa clausa*, opining that it is, in fact, a form of tabard, although he does suggest that it is 'not unlikely' that the *cappa* might also, in fact, be a 'dignified form of the tabard'.[38] On this basis he believes the chimere and the (academic) habit have a common origin: 'The black chimere has a common origin with the scarlet habit or chimere of an Oxford Doctor of Divinity. It is a form of the tabard (*tabardum* or *taberda*) or the colobbe (*collobium*) which was worn as a civil dress by persons of different classes, clerical and lay, both in England and on the Continent, but distinguished by the material, length, &c.'[39] He goes on to suggest that the *cappa clausa* was a cumbersome article of apparel, and thus clergy availed themselves of the permission to substitute the sleeveless coat, tabard or colobbe. This same substitution was made, he suggests, at the Universities of Oxford and Cambridge, although Cambridge does retain the *cappa clausa* for occasional use.

---

37 *Medieval Costume in England and France, the Thirteenth, Fourteenth and Fifteenth Centuries* (New York: Dover, 1996).

38 'The Black Chimere of Anglican Prelates', *Transactions of the St Paul's Ecclesiological Society*, 4 (1900), pp. 181–22 (p. 189).

39 Ibid., p. 188.

The 1908 report[40] follows Robinson in connecting the historical origin of the chimere with the tabard and *collobium*, essentially an overcoat. It also recognizes that a wider range of colours was used, including green, violet and murrey, and not limited to just scarlet and black.

W. H. Pinnock[41] advances an alternative view, that the chimere is descended from the *mantelletum* of the Middle Ages. He cites multiple sources, all of whom agree that the chimere was of scarlet silk, until the reign of Elizabeth I, when Bishop Hooper objected to so gay a vestment, and thus the chimere of black satin was adopted as befitting the gravity of the episcopal office.

Percy Dearmer, in *The Ornaments of the Ministers*, takes up the idea of the chimere as an overcoat, and describes it as 'part of the episcopal walking-dress which the bishops are warned not to "intermit" by the 74th Canon of 1604; and it is always used by them as their Court-dress and in the House of Lords.'[42] He equates the episcopal chimere to the priest's gown, and advances the view that it should not be used in the liturgy, although he concedes that it might be used when priest or deacon would wear a gown: when preaching and when assisting at the offices when not officiating. He notes that while the tippet is worn with the chimere the hood should not be, but 'some bishops in the last fifty years have mistakenly added the hood,'[43] an observation which concurs with our study of the episcopal portraits.

In 1925 F. C. Eeles describes the 'ordinary dress of the English bishop' as that which had been worn for centuries, namely: 'the cassock, rochet, chimere, hood, scarf and cap',[44] and so it would appear that by that time the inclusion of the hood was expected as normal. He goes on to note that some medieval pictures appear to show the bishop wearing the hood over the chimere, but it is possible that these were pictures of academic rather than clerical habits. He suggests that in the later medieval period hood and scarf were not normally worn together; when the scarf was adopted the hood was discarded. He traces the resumption of the wearing of hoods by bishops to the example of Dr Samuel Wilberforce in the nineteenth century. Wilberforce (1805–73) was consecrated bishop of Oxford in 1845.

The Warham Guild Handbook (1932) adds an interesting complication to its description of the chimere, where it says 'Chimeres are generally made of silk for ordinary use; they may be of black silk lined with the colour appropriate to the degree of the wearer.'[45] This suggests a position which confuses the riding cloak with an academic habit, the habits of the University of Oxford being lined according to the particular degree.[46] The introduction of pleating at the back of the chimere to accommodate the increasing size of the sleeves of the rochet resulted in a garment which is very similar

---

40 Convocation of Canterbury, Upper House, *The Ornaments of the Church and its Ministers: Report of the Sub-Committee appointed February 1907* (London: SPCK, 1908).

41 *The Laws and Usages of the Church and the Clergy: Ecclesiastical Vestments, or the Ornaments of the Minister* (Cambridge: Hall & Son, 1856).

42 London: Mowbray, 1908, p. 162.

43 Ibid, p. 165

44 *The Episcopal Ornaments, an Outline* (London: The Warham Guild, 1925).

45 *The Warham Guild Handbook*, 2nd edn (London: Mowbray, 1932), p. 53.

46 Note the poetic licence taken by Peter Greenham in the McCann portrait.

to the doctoral convocation habit, as used in the University of Oxford. A further confusion arises over the fact that the chimere is the convocation dress for bishops—convocation of the church, not the university. It seems quite possible that both of these areas of confusion have given rise to the ideas that the chimere belongs with the academic hood, and that only holders of doctoral degrees can wear the scarlet chimere.

Alex Kerr, drawing on the note on medieval academic dress by F. E. Brightman printed in R. T. Günther's book on the monuments in Magdalen College, Oxford, asserts the view that the chimere was a particular form of habit, a *cappa* with two side slits for the arms, and was used (in Oxford) by 'Bachelors of Divinity and Canon Law and Doctors of Medicine and the Civil Law; the present "Convocation habit" of Doctors in Oxford and the Chimere of Bishops ...'[47] However, he also acknowledges (in a footnote) that Hargreaves-Mawdsley takes the opposite view: 'some believe that the episcopal chimere had a different origin and only late came to resemble this academic habit.'[48]

The 1911 edition of *Encyclopaedia Britannica* notes that the origin of the chimere has been the subject of much debate, the view that it is a modification of the cope has been discarded, 'and it is practically proved to be derived from the medieval tabard ... an upper garment worn in civil life by all classes of people both in England and abroad. It has therefore a common origin with certain academic robes.'[49] From the fifteenth century onwards this sleeveless tabard tended to supersede the *cappa clausa* as the out-of-doors upper garment of bishops. The article goes on to suggest that while it may have denoted academic rank, it was part of the civil costume of prelates.

The *Oxford Dictionary of the Christian Church* is even less nuanced than the above article, describing the chimere as 'a gown without sleeves, worn by Anglican bishops and doctors of divinity ... it is frequently worn at liturgical functions, but also constitutes part of episcopal full dress on important civil occasions, and of the full academic dress of those entitled to wear it.'[50]

R. A. S. Macalister (1896) proposes yet another theory. Acknowledging the chimere to be 'one of the greatest puzzles to be found in the subject of vestments', he goes on to suggest that this short coat 'could be a modification of the cope or almuce—possibly a combination of the two vestments'.[51] He also holds the view of Pinnock (see above) that it is the English version of the *mantelletum*.

While there is no agreement on the precise nature of the connection between the chimere and the academic gown, there is a general agreement that the chimere originated as an upper layer of outdoor dress. It may indeed be the case that there is a common origin in the medieval tabard, but a divergence of practice from an early stage. The introduction of a yoke, due to the increasing size of sleeves on the rochet in the seventeenth century, certainly brought convergence in contemporary styles of both

---

47 'Layer upon Layer: The Evolution of Cassock, Gown, Habit and Hood as Academic Dress', *TBS*, 5 (2005), pp. 42–58 (p. 44).

48 Ibid, p. 44, fn. 11.

49 'Chimere', in *Encyclopaedia Britannica* (1911), p. 164.

50 *Oxford Dictionary of the Christian Church*, 4th edn, edited by Andrew Louth, F. L. Cross and Elizabeth A. Livingstone (Oxford: Oxford University Press, 2022), p. 330.

51 *Ecclesiastical Vestments: Their Development and History* (London: Elliot Stock, 1896), p. 199.

garments, furthering the confusion. However, the earliest examples of the outdoor cloak were commonly worn with a hood, and on that basis it would seem somewhat illogical to object to the use of the hood over the chimere today. To restrict the scarlet chimere to use with doctoral hoods only would seem to reinforce the erroneous conflation of the ecclesiastical and the academic.

Conclusion

How long does is take for a custom to become hallowed by tradition? In ecclesiastical terms the practice often precedes a change in canon law, as it did, for example, with the legalization of stoles in the Church of Ireland in 1972. Until the canons of the church were altered by the vote of General Synod, stoles were technically illegal, though their use had become quite widespread.[52] The granting of canonical permission was the result of that change in practice. The wearing of an academic hood over a chimere is not, as we have seen, subject to canon law, but merely to custom and tradition. There is clear evidence of the wearing of the hood and chimere by archbishops of Armagh for a period of at least 120 years, and the fact that this was recorded in formal portraits lends weight to the normativity of this practice. It is entirely possible that this tradition has a longer pedigree, because Marcus Gervais Beresford (the later of the two archbishops Beresford), who occupied the primatial see for a further twenty-four years, chose to be painted in the mantle of the prelate of the Order of St Patrick, but it is unlikely that this would have been worn with any regularity in a liturgical setting. It is also possible that hoods have been worn before and since, but not on every occasion and thus not seen as essential to a portrait.

It is likely that recent practice has changed for two reasons, one being that several primates have not held doctoral degrees (and the erroneous belief that only a doctoral hood should be worn over a chimere) and the other being a general decline of sartorial standards along with a more informal approach to liturgy amongst many of the clergy (of the Church of Ireland) which is leading to the abandonment not just of the hood, but of all forms of vestments and vesture, except on the most formal of occasions, in an increasing number of parishes and dioceses.

Apart from the issue of tradition, it has been established through the illustrations in Norris (and Robinson) that the hood was worn over the chimere in the twelfth century and later, as a practical outdoor garment, and thus logically as both have migrated indoors and become established clerical vesture, it seems reasonable to suggest that there is no reason they should not continue to be worn together.

The final question is a more vexing one, namely which hoods can or should be worn? If the episcopal chimere is to be understood as a variant of the doctoral convocation dress, then it would appear reasonable to suggest that only a doctoral hood is appropriate, but if it is recognized to be nothing more than a medieval 'overcoat' then it would appear that any hood could be worn. From an aesthetic point of view the black chimere, which appears to be enjoying something of a revival, is certainly a most comely garment for any hood to be worn over, while the scarlet chimere might not be

---

52 While, as we have observed, bishops enjoy a particularly non-restrictive canon, formal portraits such as we have been considering tend towards conservative choices of apparel. It is not unusual for a bishop to push the canonical and traditional boundaries in places where this would be less contentious.

so kind to the multiplicity of colours and designs now appearing, and of course it can no longer be taken for granted that doctors wear scarlet!

Acknowledgement

Photos from the Burgon Society Archive by Chris Williams.

List of Portraits

Arranged by date of the paintings.

Emily C. Way (*c.* 1847–after 1906), Portrait of Robert Knox, Archbishop of Armagh, 1893. Three-quarter length, oil on canvas, 54.5" x 42.5".

English School, late 19th century, Portrait of Primate Gregg, Archbishop of Armagh, 1894. Half length, framed as an oval, oil on canvas, 28.75" x 23.75".

Walter Frederick Osborne (1859–1903), Portrait of Primate Alexander, Archbishop of Armagh, 1893. Half length, framed as an oval, oil on canvas, 28.5" x 23.5".

Harry R. Douglas (1862–1934), Portrait of William Alexander, Bishop of Derry and Raphoe 1867–96, Archbishop of Armagh and Primate of All Ireland 1896–1911. Three-quarter length, oil on canvas, 55" x 42.5".

Frederick Whiting (1874–1951), Portrait of J. B. Crozier, Archbishop of Armagh, 1911. Half length, framed in an oval, oil on canvas, 28.5" x 24".

Mark Milbanke (1875–1927), Portrait of John B. Crozier, 1920. Three-quarter length, oil on canvas, 54.5" x 24.5".

Frederick Whiting (1874–1951), Portrait of C. F. D'Arcy, Archbishop of Armagh, 1920. Half length, oval, oil on canvas, 27.75" x 23".

Sir John Lavery (1856–1941), Portrait of Most Rev. Charles Frederick D'Arcy, MA, DD 1859-1938, Archbishop of Armagh and Primate of All Ireland, 1928. Oil on canvas.

Sir Oswald Birley (1880–1951), Portrait of John George Fitzmaurice Day. Half length, oil on canvas, 38" x 31.75".

Frank McKelvey (1875–1974), Portrait of John Allen Fitzgerald Gregg, Archbishop of Armagh, Primate of All Ireland, 1939. Half length, oil on canvas, 39" x 33".

Peter Greenham RA (1909–92), Portrait of James McCann, Archbishop of Armagh, 1959. Three-quarter length, oil on canvas, 36" x 32".

Basil Blackshaw (1932–2016), Portrait of George Otto Simms, Archbishop of Armagh, 1969. Half length, oil on canvas, 28.75" x 25".

English School, late 20th century, Portrait of John Ward Armstrong, Archbishop of Armagh, 1980. Half length, oil on canvas, 35" x 29".

Mary Dugdale U.S.W.A., Portrait of Robin Eames, Archbishop of Armagh, 1986. Three-quarter length, oil on canvas, 38" x 30".

Authors

Bruce Christianson, MSc (Victoria, NZ), DPhil (Oxon), FNZMS, FBS, is Emeritus Professor of Informatics at the University of Hertfordshire, where he taught for over thirty years. His most recent article, with Philip Goff in Volume 22, unfolded the dress of Doctors of Philosophy at the University of London. Bruce is a Foundation Fellow of the Burgon Society, and was Dean of Studies from 2003 to 2016. His grandmother knew Kate Edger (see p. 23).

Philip Goff, BD (London), AKC, FSA, FBS, Hon. Fellow, Univ. Portsmouth, is a founder and was the first Chairman of the Burgon Society. He has been associated with academical and ecclesiastical robemaking since he was a teenager and was Academic Consultant to Ede & Ravenscroft Ltd for ten years. More recently he was Area Dean of West Haringey and Vicar of St Augustine's Church, Highgate, London until retirement in 2015 and previously Senior Practice Counsellor at Clapham Family Practice. His previous article, in Volume 21, examined academic dress at the University of Portsmouth, and his history of the Society, *Hoods by the Armful*, was published as a special issue of Volume 20.

Nicholas Groves, MA, BMus, PhD (Wales), MA (EAng), BA (Lond), PGDip (York), FRHistS, FBS, was Director of the Centre for Parish Church Studies in Norwich and a freelance lecturer and writer. He was previously an Associate Tutor in Continuing Education at UEA. His previous articles, in Volume 22, covered the academic dress of the University of York, and the robes of degrees in Music at the University of London. He was the editor of *Shaw's Academical Dress* and the author of many papers and books, including the biography *Charles Franklyn: A Man of Strong Opinions*. A Foundation Fellow of the Society and Dean of Studies from 2000 to 2003, Nicholas Groves died on 29 June 2023.

Andrew Plant, BA (Leeds), PhD (Birmingham), FBS, is a pianist and musicologist, who also studied in London. His work as an accompanist to solo singers has focussed particularly on twentieth-century English repertoire, with appearances in the UK, France, Slovenia, Russia, and Bavaria. His PhD was completed during his years as a specialist at the Britten–Pears Foundation, where the historical connections around the Aldeburgh circle contributed to his FBS dissertation on Sussex, on which his article is based.

Samuel Teague, BA (Bangor), MSt (Oxon), DipABRSM, FBS, is a musician and musicologist based in Oxford, where he has undertaken postgraduate study and sung as a lay clerk with the Choir of The Queen's College for the past five years. He is currently completing his DPhil in music, at The Queen's College, focusing on Captain Henry Cooke (d. 1672), sometime Master of the Children of the Chapel Royal. His interest in academical dress was initially drawn from the intersection of such ornaments and the vestments which are worn by collegiate and cathedral choirs.

Edward Teather is reading for a BA in Social Sciences (Philosophy and Politics) at the University of Manchester. He was on the student committee of Hulme Hall, the University's oldest hall of residence, where gowned formal dinners introduced him to academic dress. He is currently on the editorial board of the University of Manchester's undergraduate politics journal, *Juncture*.

Peter Thompson, BA (QUB), MMus (Bangor), MPhil (TCD), DMin (Golden State), FBS, FGCM, FLCM, LTCL, ARIAM, is Archdeacon of Armagh, Rector of Donaghmore and Donaghmore Upper, and Assistant Organist of Armagh Cathedral. He is a member of the General Synod and the Liturgical Advisory Committee, and has edited a hymnal for the Church of Ireland. He is a Governor of the Armagh Robinson Library and of Armagh Observatory and Planetarium.

Burgon Society Shop

To shop online, visit **burgon.org.uk/shop**.

To pay post by for deliveries to the US and Canada, you may order in two ways. You pay through a PayPal invoice (in US Dollars) by writing to slw53@columbia.edu; or you may send your order with a cheque payable to The Burgon Society to:

Stephen Wolgast
University of Kansas
1435 Jayhawk Boulevard
Lawrence, Kansas 66045-7594
USA

All prices include postage and packing to the UK (if ordered through the online shop), US, and Canada (using either method).

Books

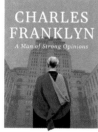

Charles Franklyn: A Man of Strong Opinions
By Nicholas Groves
Published in 2022. Soft cover. 127 pages. Perfect binding, with colour photographs.

A biography traces Franklyn's life and work, together with his contributions to academic dress and heraldry, including his designs of hoods and gowns for several universities and other organisations.
Members £12.99; Non-members £17.32

Hoods by the Armful: Academic Dress and the Founding of the Burgon Society
By Philip Goff
Published in 2021 by the Burgon Society as a history of its formation and early days. Soft cover. 113 pages. A5, perfect binding, with colour photographs.

Recollections of the people who were there at the beginning. Includes photos from the first Congregation, at Charterhouse in London in 2000.
Members £5.63; Non-members £7.50

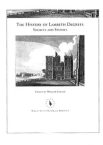

The History of Lambeth Degrees: Sources and Studies
Edited by William Gibson
Published in 2019 by the Burgon Society as the second in a series of important texts on the history of academic dress and related topics. Hardback. 200 pages.

The book brings together ten important sources and articles on the nature of Lambeth degrees and their academical dress. It includes the complete text of Bishop Francis Gastrell's legal claim in 1717 that Lambeth degrees were not equivalent to university degrees; a complete list of Lambeth degree recipients 1539–1995; an examination of Charles Franklyn's claim that the degrees are really 'state' or royal degrees; reprints of articles by Noel Cox, FBS, and by Graham Zellick, FBS, on the robes for the degrees.

Members £18.74; Non-members £24.99

Ackermann's Costumes of the Universities of Oxford and Cambridge
Edited by Nicholas Jackson
Published in 2016 by the Burgon Society as the first in its historical reprint series on academic dress and related topics. Hardback. 84 pages. Includes 37 plates (34 colour, 3 B&W).

Here are reprinted all the plates of academic dress that appeared in Rudolph Ackermann's two-volume histories of the Universities of Oxford and Cambridge published in 1814 and 1815, giving a valuable snapshot of the academic and official dress in use at these Universities at the beginning of the nineteenth century.

Members £18.74; Non-members £24.99

Shaw's Academical Dress of Great Britain and Ireland, *3rd edition, Volume I*
Edited by Nicholas Groves
Published in 2011 by the Burgon Society. Crown Quarto, bound, soft cover. 450 pages.

This new, much expanded edition is almost twice as long as the 1995 edition, incorporates a comprehensive introduction, includes newly redrawn diagrams of all the various shapes and patterns of gowns and hoods, photographs of common patterns of brocade and styles of lace and braid, and historical notes on the evolution of modern academical dress. The specifications themselves take up nearly 400 pages and are the result of several years' careful research. Also included is a bibliography of further sources.

Members £20.63; Non-members £27.50

Shaw's Academical Dress of Great Britain and Ireland, *3rd edition, Volume II: Non-Degree-Awarding Bodies*
Edited by Nicholas Groves
Published in 2014 by the Burgon Society. Crown Quarto, bound, soft cover. 236 pages.

This second volume of Shaw's Academical Dress completes the cataloguing of academic dress in Great Britain and Ireland. Whereas the first volume dealt with degree-awarding institutions (largely universities), this volume deals with non-degree awards,

On-line Bibliography

The aim is to build up a comprehensive resource for those researching the design, history and practice of academical dress.

The Introduction is a brief survey of the key materials on academical dress that are either in print or available in the larger public and university libraries.

The Alphabetical list that follows is intended to cover what has been published on the subject since the beginning of the nineteenth century; earlier items are listed if they include engravings that provide important evidence of robes of the period.

The bilbliography grows every year. Suggestions for additions (or corrections) are welcome. Please send e-mails to: webmaster@burgon.org.uk.

Find a list of books and articles to help your research at www.burgon.org.uk /research/bibliography

---

such as diplomas and certificates (where they have not already been dealt with in the first volume), and also with membership robes. As with the first volume, this volume includes diagrams of all the various shapes and patterns of gowns and hoods, photographs of common patterns of brocade and styles of lace and braid, and a bibliography of further sources.

Members £13.88; Non-members £18.50

Key to the Identification of Academic Hoods of the British Isles, *4th edition*
By Nicholas Groves
Published in 2010 by the Burgon Society. A5, comb bound. 65 pages.
Members £8.00; Non-members £12.00

Malachite and Silver: Academic Dress of the University of Stirling
By Colin Fleming
Published in 2009 by the Burgon Society. A5, stapled.
Members £6; Non-members £8

Available online only

The Academic Robes of Saint David's College, Lampeter, 1822–1971

By Nicholas Groves

To celebrate the bicentennial of the founding of the College in 2022, this revised edition of Groves' study of the history of Lampeter robes covers the BA, BD, and LD. £9.95

Guides to the academic dress of: Oxford Brooks University, the University of Wales, the University of Bath. £4.95 each

Visit burgon.org.uk/shop to place an order.

Journal

From the *Transactions'* first volume in 2001 until its fourth volume in 2004, it was called *The Burgon Society Annual*. Since 2005 it has held its present title.

Transactions of the Burgon Society   *Crown Quarto format*
Volume 23 (2023)   Further copies of this volume are available.
Members £11.25; Non-members £15

Transactions of the Burgon Society   *Crown Quarto format*
Volume 22 (2022)   *157 pages. In memoriam: Nicholas Groves; academic dress of the University of York; robes for degrees in music of the University of London; academic dress of Doctors of Philosophy at the University of London; the Oxford Convocation habit; design and use of the Chancellor's and Pro-Chancellor's robes at the University of Dublin, Trinity College; academic dress of Finland; academic dress of the University of Bath; erratum: the use and production of academic dress in Colonial, revolutionary and federal Philadelphia.*
Members £11.25; Non-members £15

Transactions of the Burgon Society   *Crown Quarto format*
Volume 21 (2021)   *251 pages. A women's academic collar at Wellesley; ceremonial and academic attire at the University of KwaZulu-Natal; the use and production of academic dress in Colonial, revolutionary and federal Philadelphia; the use of lace on academic gowns in the U.K. and Ireland: updates and corrections; Cambridge benefactors' gowns; the 1861 reforms to academic dress of the University of London; historical hoods of Trinity College, Toronto; history of doctoral dress in Aotearoa New Zealand; origins of academic dress of the University of Bristol; academic dress of the University of Portsmouth; erratum: the lack of a theology hood at the University of the West Indies.*
Members £14.50/$18 per copy; Non-members £17/$21.50 per copy

Transactions of the Burgon Society   *Crown Quarto format*
Volume 20 (2020)   *186 pages. Official dress of universities in New Zealand; academic undress at Oxford in 1635; a study of headgear in recent use at graduation in UK universities; undergraduate dress at Cambridge and its constituent colleges; the 1690 Glasgow gown order; American degree and subject colours (1963–present); the hoods of three senior doctorates at Edinburgh; designing academic dress at Hertfordshire; the lack of a theology hood at The University of the West Indies; an alternative structure to the degrees of degrees, and a response to it.*
Hoods by the Armful is a special issue of Vol. 20 and is available separately, above.
Members £11.25; Non-members £15

Transactions of the Burgon Society   *Crown Quarto format*
Volume 19 (2019)   *206 pages. The academic dress of The Open University; of the University of Exeter; of the University of Hong Kong, 1911–1941; of Kingston University; reforms in Scottish academical dress in the 1860s; academic dress in the Middle East and the Maghreb; faculty attitudes regarding academic dress at a second Land-Grant university in the US; the degrees of degrees.*
No longer available in print.

Transactions of the Burgon Society   *Crown Quarto format*
Volume 18 (2018)   *126 pages. Academic and official dress for the University of the Arts London; faculty attitudes regarding academic dress at a Land-Grant university in the US; academic dress at Nashotah House Theological Seminary; academic dress on picture postcards in Oxford; academic dress at Eton College.*
Members £11.25; Non-members £15

Transactions of the Burgon Society   *Crown Quarto format*
Volume 17 (2017)   *126 pages. Harvard returns honorary doctors' third crow's foot; academic dress of the University of Essex; American degree colours, 1936–61; the hood of the Determining BA at Oxford; the MA full-dress gown and its use by the proctors and assessor of Oxford; an argument for wider adoption of academic dress in the Roman Catholic Church.*
Members £11.25; Non-members £15

Transactions of the Burgon Society   *Crown Quarto format*
Volume 16 (2016)   *96 pages. The source and artists of Oxford academic dress engravings identified; academic dress of the University of Bradford; academic dress in British Columbia, 1866–1966; Tailors' labels; academic dress in China, 1994–2011.*
Members £11.25; Non-members £15

Transactions of the Burgon Society   *Crown Quarto format*
Volume 15 (2015)   *96 pages. French influence on the dress of Scottish Doctors of Medicine; how academic dress is mobilized in degree ceremonies; a portrait of an early 18th Century nobleman; American degree colours; and the tradition of academic costume at Acadia University.*
Members £11.25; Non-members £15

Transactions of the Burgon Society   *Crown Quarto format*
Volume 14 (2014)   *112 pages. Articles cover the discovery of an image of a Glasgow Court member's gown; an account of receiving a Lambeth degree; the influence of the Church on the development of the trencher; academic dress at the Ionian Academy; the history of academic dress in Japan; the introduction of academic dress in China; guidelines for academic dress and colours in Spain; creating officers' robes for the University of Divinity, Melbourne; and students' writing on academic dress at Columbia University.*
No longer available in print.

Transactions of the Burgon Society   *Crown Quarto format*
Volume 13 (2013)   *144 pages. Academic dress at Kenyatta University, Kenya; academic dress in Sweden; a sumptuary law of Mary I in 1554–5; Scottish ecclesiastical dress from the Reformation to the present day; academic robes of graduates of Cambridge from the end of the eighteenth century to the present day; the development of academic dress of Oxford from 1920 to 2012.*
Members £11.25; Non-members £15

Transactions of the Burgon Society   *Crown Quarto format*
Volume 12 (2012)   *128 pages. The issue includes a memoriam of Dr John Birch, who served as President of the Burgon Society from the Society's foundation in 2001 until October 2011. It also reports on academic dress of the University of Glasgow; the conservation of a nineteenth-century student gown of the University of Glasgow by the Hunterian; the dress of rectors at Scottish universities; Queen's College Oxford and purple as the blood of the Lord; gowns worn by MAs in early-seventeenth-century England and Thomas Thornton's curious sleeves; a survey of variation in US academic dress and a system of categories for departures; and a study on the history and use of lace in academic gowns in the UK and Ireland.*
Members £12.50/$15.50 per copy; Non-members £15/$19 per copy

Transactions of the Burgon Society   *Crown Quarto format*
Volume 11 (2011)   *112 pages. Academic dress in Canterbury; academic dress of the University of Hull; academic dress of the University of Leicester; the demise of 'faculty' meanings in US hoods; revisions to the academic dress of the University of Malta.*
No longer available in print.

Transactions of the Burgon Society   *Crown Quarto format*
Volume 10 (2010)   *128 pages.   This issue includes articles on the history of the Scottish undergraduate scarlet gown; Walter Pope's successful fight against the abolition of academical dress at Oxford in 1658; the robes for new doctorates at Oxford, 1895-1920; the debate on proposed academical dress for the Royal Institute of British Architects. 1923–24; and an investigation into the perceived decline of academical dress—and how this trend might be reversed or abated—by tracing the social and cultural forces that have acted upon the tradition in the last hundred years.*
Members £9.75; Non-members £13

Transactions of the Burgon Society   *Crown Quarto format*
Volume 9 (2009) — Special North American Issue   *224 pages.   Three studies on the Intercollegiate Code of Academic Costume, its development and departures from it; three covering the history and use of robes at Harvard, Princeton, and Columbia Universities; two on Canadian universities in Nova Scotia; an article with detailed illustrations on the making of an American doctoral gown; and a timeline of key events in the history of academic dress in North America.*
Members £15; Non-members £20

Transactions of the Burgon Society   *Crown Quarto format*
Volume 8 (2008)   *160 pages.   The academical dress of the University of Warwick; trends in the manufacture of gowns and hoods (with detailed descriptions and illustrations); the robes for the Master of Midwifery of the Worshipful Society of Apothecaries of London; the origins of the University of Wales robes; the use of the academic hood in quire; notes and corrections to Hargreaves-Mawdsley's* History of Academical Dress; *and the personal reminiscences of a life-long student of academical dress.*
No longer available in print.

Transactions of the Burgon Society   *Crown Quarto format*
Volume 7 (2007)   *144 pages. Academical dress at the University of Toronto; the question of Lambeth degree holders and the University of London; Wills's cigarette cards of university hoods and gowns; the robes of the medical Royal Colleges; and academic attire as a component of the livery of the Chapel Royal.*
Members £9.00/$11.50 per copy; Non-members £12.50/$16 per copy

Transactions Online Resource for Researchers

While the Burgon Society shares articles published in *Transactions of the Burgon Society* on its web site, researchers unfamiliar with the journal can find its topics through targeted searches in scholarly databases.

Open access publishing makes the *Transactions'* articles available through New Prairie Press at no cost and with few restrictions. Digital object identifiers make authors' work easily discoverable in academic searches, with the result of researchers (and the curious) downloading nearly 1,500 articles per month, on average, in the first seven months of 2023.

Our home page on the site features a map which shows where articles have been downloaded over the previous week and which articles they were. The site is also the online home to our house style sheet. It appears on the 'information for authors' page under 'Formatting Guidelines'.

New Prairie Press, hosted by Kansas State University, offers a home for the *Transactions* and other scholarly pub-

Articles from *Transactions* are published online through a scholarly library at newprairiepress.org/burgonsociety/.

lications edited or written by scholars committed to the principles of open access publishing. The Press focuses on journals, monographs, and conference proceedings in the humanities, social sciences, and the arts.

All volumes of *Transactions of the Burgon Society*, including *The Burgon Society Annual*, have been on the New Prairie Press site since October 2016.
